INSIDE THE INSURANCE INDUSTRY

Insurance Help for Individuals and Businesses

Fourth Edition

Kevin L. Glaser

CPCU, CIC, SCLA, ARM, AAI, AIC, ARM-P, AIS

Revised © 2025 Right Side Creations, LLC, Oconomowoc, Wisconsin. All rights reserved.

ISBN 978-0-9910388-8-6

Printed in the United States of America.

Front and back cover artwork, design and wording created by Briana R. Brandt.

Book design assistance provided by Heidi Sutherlin.

Limit of Liability/Disclaimer of Warranty:

The information contained in this book is based on the author's own opinions and is not intended to be legal or accounting advice, or any type of expert assistance. This work is sold with the understanding that neither the author nor the publisher is engaged in rendering legal, accounting, insurance advice, or other professional services or advice. The advice and strategies contained herein may not be suitable for every situation. Each individual's circumstances may be different. For that reason, the reader is solely responsible for obtaining advice from a legal or accounting expert.

The author and the publisher make no representations or warranties with respect to the accuracy or completeness of the contents of this work and specifically disclaim all warranties, including without limitation warranties of fitness for a particular purpose. No warranty may be created or extended by sales or promotional materials. Neither the publisher nor the author shall be liable for damages arising from your use or reliance upon any information contained in this book. Your use and/or reliance upon any information contained in this work is solely and exclusively at your own risk.

The work may reference third-party organizations or data. Such references or citations does not mean that the author or the publisher endorses the information or the source of such information. Readers should be aware that information contained in the contents of this publication continually changes, and may have changed between when this work was written and when it is read. Such information may be out-of-date, no longer relevant, or no longer applicable to the topics contained in the work.

No part of this publication may be reproduced, stored in a retrieval system, or transmitted in any form or by any means, electronic, mechanical, photocopying, recording, scanning, or otherwise, except as permitted under section 107 or 108 of the 1976 United States copyright act, without the prior written permission of the author and publisher. Requests to the publisher for permission should be addressed to Right Side Creations, LLC, 1343 N. Riverline Drive, Oconomowoc, WI, 53066.

Contents

About the Author i
    Products Offered by Right Side Creations, LLC iv

Acknowledgements vii

Prologue ix

1. The Importance of Managing Risk 1
    The Risk Process 2

2. The Inner Workings of Insurance Companies 5
    Types of Insurance Companies 6
        Insurance Carrier Structural Advantages and Disadvantages 7
    Methods of Distribution 8
    Insurance Agents vs. Insurance Brokers 10
    Bid-Rigging in the Insurance Marketplace 11

3. Insurance Company Internal Department Functions 15
    Marketing 15
        External Sales 16
        Internal Sales and Marketing 16
        The Insurance Sales Process 17
        Insurance Company Incentives 18
    Insurance Agent Duties 20
    Insurance Purchaser Duties 21
    Claims 23
        Resources Used by Adjusters 24

  Adjuster Duties Owed to Policyholders 24
  Ambiguous Policy Wording Example 26
  Why Claims Settlements Can Be Difficult to Understand 27
  Questions and Answers Related to Payment of Claims 29
 Underwriting 37
 Policy Services 39
 Audit Department 40
 Loss Control 41

4. Other Insurance Company Support Positions 45
 Legal 45
 Actuary 46
  The Real Scoop on Actuarial Changes 48
 Subrogation 49
  Steps in the Subrogation Process 50
  Heightened Insurance Carrier Focus on Subrogation 51
 Internal Audit 52
 Product Development 53
 Information Technology 55
 Management 56
  Unforeseen Circumstances Impacting Insurers 57

5. A Little-Known Factor Affecting Insurance Companies 61
 Reinsurance 61
  How Reinsurance Works 62
  The Impact of Reinsurance on Insurance Market Cycles 64

6. External (Third-Party) Resources 67
 Public Adjusters 67
 Insurance Consultants 68

Exposure Analysis and Recommendations 69
Other Specialized Services 69

7. Insurance Litigation 71
Bad Faith 73
First-Party and Third-Party Bad Faith Claims 74
Sample Litigation Engagements 75

8. Pricing 81
Special Pricing Tools Used for Business Policies 83
Introducing IRPMs 84
Why Your Business May Not Be Desirable to an Insurer 86
Your Mindset Matters When Saving Money 87

9. How to Get the Best Insurance Deal 89
Be Cautious When Purchasing Insurance Without an Agent 90
Two Very Important Areas When Quoting Insurance 92
Specific Steps to Decrease What is Paid for Insurance 93
Introducing the RISC Analyzer 99
Perhaps An Insurance Consultant Can Help 100
How Much Does an Insurance Agent Earn? 101

10. More on Risk Management 105
Risk Manager Essential Responsibilities 107

11. Evolving Areas in the Insurance Industry 111

12. The Future of Insurance 117
Insurance Jobs That May Be Less Impacted by AI 117

Epilogue 123

Appendix 127

How a Consultant Looks at a Business Risk 127

Western Wooden Products, Inc. 128

Western Wooden Products Year-End Financial Statement 130

    Case Analysis Questions 131

    Case Analysis Worksheet* 132

Western Wooden Products, Inc. Year-End Financial Answers 133

Sample 2: Insurance Proposal Comparison Worksheet 137

    Insurance Proposal Comparison 138

Index 145
If More Help is Needed 157

About the Author

Kevin L. Glaser is president of Risk & Insurance Services Consulting, LLC (**RISC**), a fee-only property and casualty consulting business located in Oconomowoc, Wisconsin.

RISC serves businesses, government entities, and affluent individuals by providing professional services such as litigation support and expert witness testimony; complex insurance program design; negotiation of insurance coverages and pricing; development, implementation and monitoring of contractual risk transfer agreements; internal audits of existing insurance and risk management programs; agency and insurance company effectiveness reviews; development of unique bid templates to test the marketplace; analysis of worker's compensation programs, and the review of claims payments and claim control practices.

Mr. Glaser has worked for both mutual and stock insurance carriers, including for a subsidiary of a large multinational insurance company based out of Great Britain.

He has worked in a wide variety of carrier positions including: Property Adjuster; Field Underwriter; Personal Lines District Manager; Commercial Lines District Manager, Territory Manager and Territorial Business Manager. Glaser has first-hand experience in personal lines, commercial lines, farm lines, working with affluent family accounts, and providing long-term risk management services to the State of Wisconsin as a Risk Management Specialist.

Mr. Glaser's responsibilities have included overseeing results for business insurance departments and personal insurance departments, as well as ratemaking and management of underwriters and support staff. In addition, he was a select member of a reinsurance-driven, company-wide consulting project whose mission was to re-engineer the existing internal structure of an insurance company that he worked for.

Mr. Glaser has a B.A. from Creighton University in Omaha, Nebraska, and has earned several distinguished professional insurance designations including: Chartered Property and Casualty Underwriter (CPCU); Certified Insurance Counselor (CIC); Senior Claim Law Associate (SCLA); Associate in Risk Management (ARM); Accredited Advisor in Insurance (AAI); Associate in Claims (AIC); Associate in Risk Management-Public Entities (ARM-P); and Associate in Insurance Services (AIS). He has been quoted in national news publications such as *The Wall Street Journal, The Milwaukee Journal Sentinel*, and *The Hartford Courant* relative to insurance issues.

Mr. Glaser has provided litigation support services in nearly sixty cases, divided almost evenly between plaintiff and defense attorney cases. He has worked with insurance carrier Error and Omission writers, as well as attorney-focused expert services firms.

He was recognized as a recommended insurance expert service provider by the A.M. Best Company for over a decade. Litigation support services include the areas of commercial and personal property and casualty insurance, including insurance policy review; coverage interpretations; assistance with pre-discovery strategies; review of denied claims to determine whether coverage might exist; detailed research; trial testimony; and providing second opinions by reviewing key legal focus areas and identifying additional areas that may have been overlooked.

Glaser has served as an associate faculty member of the nationally recognized *National Alliance for Insurance Education & Research*, now known as the *Risk & Insurance Education Alliance* (sponsor of the Society of Certified Insurance Counselor courses), and was approved to teach a variety of insurance-related courses related to business insurance coverages throughout the USA.

Additionally, Glaser taught an insurance-related course for the business school of the University of Wisconsin-Whitewater, which is ranked among the top 50 business schools in the USA. He has also provided long-term risk management services for the University of Wisconsin-Milwaukee.

Mr. Glaser is a national speaker in the areas of insurance and risk management, presenting to diverse groups such as *Corporate Casual*, a professional association comprising accountants, attorneys, and bankers; *The COSBE (Council of Small Business Executives) Group*; *NAPFA (the National Association of Personal Financial Advisors); MRA (Management Association); SHERM (Society for Human Resource Management);* and *TEC (The Executive Committee)*, an international group of CEOs.

PRODUCTS OFFERED BY RIGHT SIDE CREATIONS, LLC

Books

- *Inside the Insurance Industry*
- *Inside the Insurance Industry–Second Edition*
- *Inside the Insurance Industry–Third Edition*
- *Inside the Insurance Industry–Fourth Editon*
- *The Great Tompall: Forgotten Country Music Outlaw*

Risk Management Software

The **RISC Analyzer**©™ Exposure Identification Software

BOOK ORDER FORM

Are you a "classic country" fan? Here's a biography about the Outlaw Tompall Glaser, written by his nephew, that you won't want to miss!

The Great Tompall: Forgotten Country Music Outlaw by Kevin L. Glaser Hardcover, 6" x 9" 364 pages with more than two dozen images

Order your copy from Right Side Creations, LLC by calling 262-569-0929, visiting our online store at www.rtsidecreations.com or by completing this form and sending your check or money order by mail.

PLEASE PRINT   Today's Date: _____

Your Name: _____

Address: _____

City/State/ZIP: _____

E-mail: _____

Quantity: _____   *The Great Tompall* @ $29.95 = _____

Ship to: ☐ Same as above   Shipping: _____

                                 5.1% Sales Tax if WI resident: _____

                                           Total Amt. Enclosed: _____

If shipping to a different address:

Your Name: _____

Address: _____

City/State/ZIP: _____

Shipping: $6.50 first book. $2.25 each additional book. We ship by Priority Mail within contiguous USA only. Contact us for international shipping rates or other options.

<u>Mail payment with order form to</u>:
Right Side Creations, LLC
1343 N Riverline Dr.
Oconomowoc, WI 53066-6910

Acknowledgements

There are a great many people who deserve my thanks and appreciation for providing guidance and assistance to me throughout my professional career. However, there are none more deserving of my endearing gratitude than my immediate family.

More than thirty years ago my wife, my two-year-old son and I moved several hundred miles from our hometown in Nebraska to Wisconsin. We left behind friends and family for a new adventure and had no one to rely upon but ourselves. First and foremost, I wish to thank my wonderful wife for her endless support throughout four decades of marriage. She willingly moved to a new home in a faraway state, encouraged me to start an insurance and risk management consulting business from scratch, and has been the rock upon whom I have leaned for so many years. She continues to be the person I rely upon more than anyone else, and I am blessed to have her in my life.

I am also grateful to my oldest son for the many special talents that he shares with me and the rest of our family. He has also chosen the insurance industry as his profession, and is one of the most learned persons in this industry. He earned a master of science in insurance management and, at last count, he has amassed 60 professional insurance-related designations. I believe this is more than anyone else and if this title was listed in the Guinness Book of World Records, I am certain he would be a contender for the top spot. He was also the impetus for me to publish my initial edition of *Inside the Insurance Industry* and without him, that book would never have been published.

My second child has also chosen the insurance industry to earn a living and to make his mark. He has earned a master of engineering in risk engineering and system analytics, along with his CPCU designation, to assist in his career path. He has a natural ability to look at things differently than many others and I appreciate his insights when we discuss various insurance situations. He has worked for large insurance brokerages and insurance carriers, and has underwritten some of the largest property-driven accounts in the USA and overseas.

My oldest daughter adds perspectives outside the realm of insurance and deserves my thanks and gratitude due to her multiple talents, which she freely shares with me and our entire family. She is a talented singer and musician, and she is making her mark as a senior project manager for a cloud-based payroll and human resources software company. Her various abilities allow me to step outside of the insurance and risk management world, reminding me of the importance of living a well-rounded life.

And last, I am appreciative of my youngest child for her quick wit, natural intelligence, musical skills, and her good common sense. And, surprise, she also works in the insurance industry! She is currently a business analyst specializing in user-centered design, and has earned her Master of Science in Information Design and Strategy from a prestigious midwestern university. She also possesses artistic abilities as evidenced by her book cover artwork for my prior book, *Inside the Insurance Industry–Third Edition*, as well as her front and back cover designs for *Inside the Insurance Industry–Fourth Edition*.

Prologue

In my more than thirty-five years spent working in various capacities within the insurance industry, I have witnessed many changes. One thing that has not changed is the confusion surrounding insurance products that are sold to customers. The operative word in the last sentence is "sold."

It continues to amaze me how little individuals and decision-makers at businesses know about the insurance products that they purchase. Thousands of dollars, hundreds of thousands of dollars and even several million dollars are spent to buy property and casualty insurance policies, yet buyers do not fully understand what they are spending their money on. Insurance is sold and decisions are made based upon factors such as the insurance agent's looks, his or her presentation abilities, the relationships between parties, and so forth. Yet, these things have little to do with the true reason insurance should be bought.

An insurance policy is a contract between the insurance company and the individual or business that purchases its product. The insurance policy is a promise—a promise to pay by either reimbursing you (property losses) or paying on your behalf (liability losses) if a specific occurrence takes place that is covered under the policy, subject to policy provisions, such as conditions, limitations, and exclusions. Therefore, it is imperative that buyers of insurance understand how insurance companies work, the way insurance products are developed, how insurance is sold, how claims are handled, the insured's (you are the insured) legal rights under the insurance policy, and much more.

I fully understand that most people do not want to spend a lot of time thinking about the topic of insurance. However, by taking a "head in the sand" approach, consumers allow insurance companies complete control over several aspects of the insurance process, and this need not be the case.

Simply put: it is in your best interest to educate yourself about insurance. No matter how much money you pay for insurance it is likely a significant dollar amount in your overall budget. Thus, you ought to know what you are getting for your money and should understand the rights you are afforded under the insurance contract.

My intent in writing each edition of my *Inside the Insurance Industry* books has been to share with you the inner workings of the insurance industry. And, as a result, to help you make educated insurance purchasing decisions and to gain a better understanding of how you can proactively address issues that may arise within the provisions of your insurance policies.

But please understand that this book is not intended to be a "hatchet job" on the insurance industry. Rather, my purpose is to shed light upon an industry that is not understood by a great number of people. The fact that facets of the insurance business are conducted in particular ways, including profit-sharing agreements and other ways of earning money, does not in and of itself mean that those working within the insurance industry are untrustworthy or otherwise bad people. After all, other industries have their own secrets concerning how they provide incentives to their internal sales staff or external distribution chain, such as the holdbacks given by car manufacturers to their dealers.

Nonetheless, the information provided in this book should help guide you in making some decisions about your insurance purchases. I believe in the axiom "the more you know, the better off you will be." Hopefully, you will find that I have met this goal after reading *Inside the Insurance Industry– Fourth Edition*.

Clarification: It would be too onerous to include state-specific information throughout this book, so the State of Wisconsin has frequently been used as a geographic reference for sake of consistency. And while Wisconsin situations mentioned apply to most other states, please discuss any state-specific questions with an agent, broker, or consultant.

1.

The Importance of Managing Risk

Risk. This single word is tossed around by many different industries and occupations, and its meaning varies somewhat, depending on how it is used.

Financial advisors warn that there is a risk of loss when you invest in a stock, a mutual fund or other financial product. Banks warn of interest rate risk. Governments warn of risk of inflation, risk of war, and more. Pharmaceutical companies warn of risks associated with a drug's possible adverse reactions. And this is just the tip of the proverbial iceberg.

It seems that risk is involved in *everything*, and there is truth to this statement. If you choose to get out of bed in the morning, there is a possibility that you may be injured in some manner. You may slip and fall in your house or somewhere else during the day. You may be injured in a car accident. You may catch an illness from someone that you come into close contact with during the day. Or any number of other negative events may happen to you once you leave the confines of your bed.

But it is unrealistic to stay in bed every day of your life–and staying in bed brings its own set of risks, such as possible onset of heart disease due to a lack of exercise. Also, what a sad life this would be! So, each of us ventures out of our beds at some point each day, exposing ourselves to a variety of potentially adverse risks.

For my purpose in this book, I will define risk simply as "risk of loss." And risk management is, as you likely guessed, the management of risk. Pretty simple so far, but make no mistake–risk management is quite complex once you delve into this concept.

There are many definitions of risk management that I have come across in my career, and one decent definition was developed by Robert J. Marshburn, CRM, CIC, ARM. Mr. Marshburn defined risk management as "the practice of protecting an organization from financial harm by identifying, analyzing and controlling risk at the lowest possible cost." But I have amended this definition somewhat to encompass *personal risk* in addition to organizational (business) risk, and *reasonableness of cost*, so the working definition of risk management I will use going forward is:

Protection of individuals and businesses from financial harm by identifying, analyzing, and controlling risk at the lowest feasible cost.

There have been volumes written about risk management, but my intent here is to simply provide an overview of this process to help develop a general understanding of this important topic.

The Risk Process

The risk management process starts with *risk identification*. Before risk can be managed it must be identified. There are numerous ways to identify risks, but here are a few examples: formal questionnaires, checklists, flowcharts, organization charts and financial information.

Once risks have been identified it is important to analyze them. *Risk analysis* involves digging into and assessing these risks, including past losses that may have occurred.

Risk control involves addressing the risks that have been identified and analyzed. Risk control can take place both <u>before</u> risk outcomes ("losses") have been realized or <u>after</u> the risk outcomes have taken place. Pre-loss risk control measures include: avoidance, prevention, reduction, segregation, and transfer. Post-loss methods include claims management and disaster recovery.

Since insurance falls under pre-loss risk measures, a major focus of this book involves risk control. Some examples of pre-loss risk control include:

Avoidance

This is my favorite pre-loss risk control method. Simply put, this involves making a conscious choice not to participate in a specific activity. When I was young, I told my dad that the action I was taking hurt me. He said, "Then don't do it!" Avoidance.

Prevention

Attempting to prevent losses from occurring. For instance, a building custodian chooses to wet mop a dirty tile floor after business hours when there is no foot traffic versus during the middle of work hours. The wet floor is not walked upon and it dries prior to sustaining foot traffic the next day.

Reduction

Taking actions to reduce losses that might occur. Using the same floor mopping example found above, if the custodian is unable to wet mop after business hours and instead does so during the business day, he or she can place "danger, wet floors" warning signs at intervals where the floor is wet. By alerting people to the fact that the floor is wet, people should walk more slowly and carefully; thus, even if they slip, the extent of their injury may be reduced.

Segregation of Exposures

One example is to keep computer backups offsite (or in the cloud using cloud backups) in case there is damage to the primary location where the computer is located. Another example is to build a factory in two different locations that are geographically far away from one another rather than building two buildings directly next to one another. That way, if a tornado destroys one building, the other should be unscathed.

Transfer

Shifting the risk for certain activities to another person or business entity. Contractual transfer occurs when there is an agreement between two parties: that one party passes risks along to someone else and that other party accepts the transferred risk, usually because they are monetarily compensated to do so in some manner. For instance, a general contractor may demand that a subcontractor sign a hold harmless and/or indemnity agreement prior to doing work (and getting compensated for such work) for the general contractor.

Simply put, a hold harmless agreement protects one party from claims of legal liability from the other party, and an indemnity agreement is a contractual agreement to pay for losses or damage caused by another party.

Insurance is considered a type of indemnity agreement, and it falls under the pre-loss risk control method of transfer. Individuals and businesses *transfer* their risk of loss for certain events that may occur to insurance companies, in exchange for payment of an insurance premium. And while certain risks are transferred, this transfer is limited due to several factors, such as coverage amounts, policy limitations, exclusions, sub-limits, and more. Keep in mind that, while you may want to be covered for *everything*, this is not the purpose of insurance.

Insurance is an important mechanism that allows people to take risks. Without taking risks, there would be fewer innovations, economic growth would stagnate, and a plethora of negative outcomes would result. In short, our society would suffer. So educated risk-taking is a good thing. And having insurance policies provide financial backing for the occurrence of specific losses is a wonderful thing, indeed.

2.
The Inner Workings of Insurance Companies

Based on my personal experience, a great number of people do not understand how insurance companies operate. In fact, a reasonable argument can be made that nearly everyone working outside of the insurance industry does not have a good grasp on how insurance works.

Case in point, I served as an expert witness for the defense in a court trial focused on insurance policy language. When providing trial testimony, a significant amount of my time was spent helping the jury understand how insurance companies work. The jury was made up of twelve individuals from every walk of life. There were students, housewives, business people, retirees, and others. The one common thread was that none of them really understood even the most basic concepts about insurance.

Part of my job was to help the jury understand the insurance company distribution process, among other things. To accomplish this, I used a flip chart and compared an auto manufacturer to an insurance company.

In essence, insurance companies (also known as "insurers," "carriers" and "primary insurers") are much like car manufacturers. Both sell final products to consumers: one sells automobiles and the other insurance policies. Some common characteristics include that each industry has a product development department, both keep their eyes on their competitors, and on their existing and potential customer desires (and make product changes accordingly); and each is subject to government regulation.

Other similarities between auto manufacturers and insurance companies will be shared later in this book to help you better understand the insurance industry.

As a starting point, you must understand that insurance companies are just like all other businesses–they are focused on making a profit. Making a profit is not an inherently bad thing. It allows insurers to remain a going concern, to hire good people, pay rent and utilities, and gives them the opportunity to do things that cost money, such as introducing new products and entering new geographical territories.

But if you watch insurance company television ads you might think that they will do anything they can to make you a happy policyholder at the time of loss. Sometimes true, sometimes not. Since the insurance policy is a contract, some events are simply not covered claims under the policy. And some insurance companies look at policy wording ambiguities in their favor and deny claims accordingly, while other insurance companies have a philosophy of trying to pay claims rather than denying claims.

Types of Insurance Companies

Insurance companies are typically chartered as *mutual* or *stock* companies. A mutual company is owned by its policyholders (also referred to as "insureds"). A stock company is owned by its stockholders. There are pros and cons to each type of company charter.

What does it mean for a mutual company to be technically owned by its member policyholders? It means that members can participate in the insurance company's meetings by voting or in other ways that are determined by their board of directors and in accordance with provisions of law.

An offshoot of a pure mutual company is where a mutual holding company is formed as the parent company, along with the establishment of a stock subsidiary where 100 percent of the stock is ultimately controlled by the mutual holding company. American Family Mutual Insurance Company, headquartered in Madison, Wisconsin, underwent this change several years ago. Several reasons for making this change were cited by American Family, including offering them the ability to facilitate expansion into new states, to offer new products, and to pursue customer-driven initiatives.

Insurance Carrier Structural Advantages and Disadvantages

One advantage of a mutual company from an insurance consumer's perspective is the possibility of receiving a "refund" in the form of a policy dividend if the insurance company's profit-making results are better than anticipated. In other words, if the company makes money based upon the rate (price) it charges after paying claims and other expenses, it can refund a portion of these profits to its policyholders. Such refunds may take the form of rate reductions or maintaining current insurance product pricing.

Realistically, while the mutual companies tout their structure and state that their ability to reduce prices is a result of being owned by their policyholders, the prices they charge for their products are not necessarily lower than the prices charged by other types of insurance companies when comparisons are made on an "apples to apples" basis.

The main advantage of stock companies is that they can be priced very competitively up front because they are focused on making a profit for their stockholders. Profits that are realized are typically paid out to their stockholders and not to their insurance policyholders. Stock companies have an additional advantage in that they can sell more stock if they need to raise capital for any reason. Over the years, some mutual companies have converted to stock companies to acquire other companies, to expand their product offerings, and to grow the geographical territories where they were conducting business.

Methods of Distribution

Insurance companies can also be distinguished by the type of product distribution method they use. The three main distribution methods are: through an independent agency or brokerage, through an exclusive agency, or through a direct writer.

Insurance agencies have a dual fiduciary duty to both their customers and to the insurance companies that they represent, while insurance brokerages technically have a primary fiduciary duty to their clients. But, both agencies and brokerages place insurance policies through insurance companies that they are licensed to represent. Therefore, for ease of discussion in this section about insurance policy distribution, I will lump both together under the independent agency system. Additional information about agents and brokers will be provided later in this chapter.

Independent agents and brokers sell the products of many different insurance companies. Basically, these agencies and brokerages are privately owned (or, in the case of large brokerages, publicly owned stock companies), profit-oriented businesses, much like a single hometown location appliance store that sells several different manufacturer brand names. But in reality, many independent agencies act as "manufacturer's representatives" for insurance companies.

Using the auto manufacturer analogy, carmakers distribute their products through auto dealerships. Each dealership is individually owned and may sell various brands of cars. Manufacturers and dealerships enter contracts that detail the responsibilities of each party and manufacturers offer dealerships the opportunity to earn bonuses based upon sales numbers. Each of these characteristics also hold true for insurance companies and the agencies that operate within the independent agency system.

Independent insurance agents advertise individually, or as part of trade associations like the Professional Insurance Agents (PIA), and under the marketing umbrella of the insurance carriers they represent. Sometimes, the insurance agent and the insurance company share the cost of advertising. This type of arrangement is known as cooperative advertising, or "co-op advertising." An example of this type of arrangement is a radio, television or print advertisement for an insurance agency that represents and sells insurance for insurance carriers such as Travelers, CNA, Chubb, or a litany of other insurers.

Alternatively, exclusive agents (also referred to as "captive agents") must place business with only one insurance company (referred to as the "captive company"), but often have the flexibility to run their offices as they see fit. Agents who exclusively represent one insurance company may be considered independent contractors by the insurance company (e.g., American Family Insurance, State Farm and Nationwide) or they may be considered exclusive insurance agent employees (e.g., agents at Liberty Mutual). Many exclusive agents are restricted by contract from submitting business to any other company unless the application is first rejected by the agent's captive company.

For exclusive agencies, the marketing of insurance products is typically the responsibility of the insurance company, although some exclusive agents may be allowed to mount their own local marketing campaigns to gain name recognition in their communities.

Another method of insurance distribution involves direct writers. Here, insurance is sold by an *employee* of an insurance company directly to customers and all business must be written exclusively with that insurer. The policies sold by employee agents are owned by these insurance companies. Therefore, when employees leave, they are not entitled to take the customer with them. Examples of direct writer companies include Amica Mutual Insurance Company, Federated Mutual Insurance Company, GEICO, and USAA Direct. Sentry Insurance also has a direct writer division, but utilizes the independent insurance agency system for certain types of policyholders that it insures.

To market their insurance products, many direct writing companies use television and print advertising, telephone, web-related or mail solicitation to sell their insurance products to the public. Many times, direct writers will combine several different sales methods to market their products.

Regardless of who pays for it, the marketing of insurance products has changed over the past several years and it is constantly evolving. For example, telephone marketing was prevalent in the past. But with the advent of "do not call" lists in several states, insurance companies and agencies are now focusing on other methods. Internet marketing has seen exponential growth. Almost unheard of a few years ago, things such as blogs, website enhancements (including the tracking of visitors), X (formerly Twitter) postings (tweets), Facebook and the use of other types of social media have become commonplace. Some companies have even tested sending targeted cell phone text advertisements to potential insurance customers.

Insurance Agents vs. Insurance Brokers

Before leaving the area of insurance product distribution, it is critical that a frequent cause of consumer confusion be made clear. Some people who place insurance for their customers or clients refer to themselves as *insurance agents* and others refer to themselves as *insurance brokers*. It is important to know the difference.

Insurance agents have signed contracts to represent insurance companies and to sell the products offered by these insurance companies. As a result, legally, they have a dual fiduciary responsibility to both the insurance companies they represent and to the customers that buy the insurance policies that they sell.

Insurance brokers technically represent their customers (often referred to as clients), not insurance companies. But insurance brokerages today have signed contracts in effect with a multitude of insurance companies, just as independent insurance agencies do.

And while there remains a legal differentiation between insurance agents and insurance brokers, in practical terms there is little difference between brokers and agents from the standpoint that both procure insurance policies for purchasers of insurance.

Examples of large insurance brokers include Marsh & McLennan, Aon, Arthur J. Gallagher & Co., Willis Towers Watson (WTW), and HUB International. These brokers have office locations throughout the USA, and some have international offices, as well. Many of the larger insurance agencies are regional in scope but generally have only one or a handful of office locations. I will not name specific agencies because these may no longer exist at the time you read this book due to the considerable consolidation that has taken place in the insurance agency industry over the past several years. And it does not appear to be ending anytime soon.

So, as stated earlier, be advised that the words "agent" and "broker" will sometimes be used interchangeably in this book since both terms refer to businesses that sell policies for insurance companies.

2 | The Inner Workings of Insurance Companies

Bid-Rigging in the Insurance Marketplace

The insurance business came under scrutiny several years ago when Eliot Spitzer, then the State of New York's Attorney General, investigated a case of insurance bid-rigging. The situation in Mr. Spitzer's case involved a large insurance brokerage that was not only controlling which insurance companies would provide bids, but also the prices that the insurance companies would charge for the coverages requested. In direct conflict with a broker's legal duty to their customers, this brokerage acted only in their own best interest and in the best interest of the insurance company that they decided to do business with.

What took place was that the insurance brokerage positioned itself to receive the highest possible commissions from insurance companies by restricting the consumers' access to other insurance companies and/or by increasing the prices consumers paid. As a result of the Attorney General's investigation, the area of contingent (based upon the occurrence of a future event) commissions in the insurance industry became a matter of public concern.

Insurance companies are not alone in their bonuses paid to agents and brokers that sell their policies. For instance, auto makers often offer some type of bonus to dealerships that sell their cars. This may be in the form of a dealer holdback, or some other type of incentive. But insurance companies are held to a different standard in this regard. Contingent commissions are paid by carriers to insurance brokers and agents, generally on an annual basis, predicated upon their performance during the prior twelve-month period. These commissions are paid when certain specific criteria are met. These criteria may include things such as:

- Insurance company revenue growth (measured by standards such as insurance policies sold).
- Number growth (growth on a "per policy" basis compared to last year).

- Loss ratio results (dollars paid out in claims divided by the amount of money paid for an insurance policy. Typically, a pure loss ratio of less than 50% is desirable).

- Policy retention percentages (how many policies an insurance agency or brokerage kept in force at the date the insurance renewed. A number higher than 80% is favorable).

- Miscellaneous other factors, such as a block of insurance policies moved from one insurance carrier to another (known as a "book of business rollover"), premium growth in specific industries desired by the carrier, or at specific agency office locations where the carrier wishes to grow, and so forth.

As a result of public backlash, several large insurance agencies and brokers (but not all of them) decided to no longer accept contingent commissions.

Today, however, many of the agencies and brokers that refused to accept contingent commissions have reevaluated their position and now once again accept these payments. The reasoning behind their change of heart differs, but some agencies and brokers felt that if they fully disclose their potential to obtain contingent commission income (what they consider transparency), it was acceptable to once again enter into some type of additional commission agreements with insurance carriers.

Some insurance agencies and brokers never did stop taking bonus commission dollars and continued to accept these "enhanced commissions" from insurance carriers with the blessing of their customers. Throughout the Eliot Spitzer uproar, many consumers remained unaware of potential agency and brokerage conflicts of interest and how it might adversely impact their own insurance cost.

It is important that you understand the bid-rigging type of situation that was exposed by Eliot Spitzer in the past is *still* a concern today. Part of the reason for this is due to how insurance policies are written. Agents and brokers continue to be solely in control of which insurance companies are involved in the insurance bidding process and since they are the ones who present the final insurance proposals (containing coverages and prices) to their customers, they control which insurance company quotes are presented.

And the possibility exists that the quotes presented are not the ones in their customers' best interest from a pricing and/or coverage standpoint.

Certainly not all agents/brokers control the insurance policy quoting process by holding back information from their clients, but the methodology used to sell insurance today continues to provide the opportunity for an agent/broker to present quotes in their own best interest.

3.

Insurance Company Internal Department Functions

It is important to have at least a basic understanding of the way insurance companies do business because any one of the departments may have an adverse impact on the insurance policy that you have purchased.

The major internal departments in insurance companies are: Marketing, Claims, Underwriting, Policy Services, Audit Department and Loss Control. Other support positions include: Legal, Actuary, Subrogation, Internal Audit, Product Development, Information Technology and Management. Each of the major internal departments will be discussed separately, with other support positions addressed in Chapter 4.

Marketing

Marketing consists of both an *internal* and an *external* sales force. An internal sales force consists of the employees of the insurance company who sell to, or support, the company's chosen distribution channel. External marketing (or "sales force") sells the insurance company's products to the final customer via the individual company's chosen distribution channel. As discussed in the prior chapter, these distribution methods include independent agents, captive agents, and direct sales.

External Sales

The external sales force is comprised of the independent agency or exclusive agency agents who sell the insurance company's products. These external salespersons are often categorized as "sales" rather than "marketing," but both are involved in the process of trying to influence the ultimate decision-maker, the consumer, to buy their company's insurance product. Note that the direct writer company's marketing department fulfills both internal and external sales functions.

If independent insurance agents are used, the insurance company's marketing representatives work to convince agents who have contracts with their company that they should be selling their company's products. Where captive, or exclusive, agents are used, internal marketing provides sales assistance to the individual agent—such as training, acting as a liaison between agents and the company to help when there is a problem, and assisting in writing new insurance policies—referred to as "new accounts."

Internal Sales and Marketing

Internal marketing also keeps others in the insurance company abreast of what competing companies are doing in the marketplace, and may aid in development of new products or making changes to existing products. These changes can be either enhancements (broadening of coverages) or restrictions of coverage when it is determined that specific coverage is too broad, when too many claims are paid or claims payment dollars during a given timeframe (i.e., one year) are too high.

There are pros and cons to each method of insurance sales from a customer's point of view. As mentioned earlier, even though independent agents tout the fact that they do not work for any single insurance company, and do, in fact, have a duty to work in the best interests of their customers, they also have a fiduciary (legal) duty to each of the companies that they represent. This legal position involving a dual fiduciary duty sets the stage for possible conflicts of interest.

The Insurance Sales Process

Agents who sell the products of one company–or exclusive agents–must sell whatever is available to them via that single company, no matter how costly, or how good or bad their policy is. Companies that have chosen this method of distribution typically put much more emphasis on the sales process. The people who sell their products are well-trained salespersons who know how to sell over all types of objections.

Interestingly, many insurance agents are people who were previously well-known sports figures or who have otherwise been involved in activities that result in name recognition in the communities where they sell insurance. Consumers of insurance feel special when they rub elbows with these agents, and are proud to tell their friends and neighbors who they have purchased insurance policies from.

While insurance agencies can operate differently when it comes to hiring new agents, it is not uncommon for them to require their new agents to have somewhere between 100 to 1,000 business and/or individual insurance *leads* to contact prior to starting an insurance sales career path if they lack consumer name recognition.

Once someone is hired as an insurance agent and the initial 100 to 1,000 leads have been exhausted, how can the agent generate additional leads? There are several methods. Leads can be purchased from outside companies who specialize in this sort of thing. Or, they can come about due to advertising. However, the most popular method is to develop and work from a list of referrals. Referrals come about when a person or business seeks out an agent based on positive things they have heard about the person, or when one of the agent's existing customers provides the name of a friend or business associate to the agent. In a best-case scenario, the insurance agent's existing customers pave the way for the agent to contact their personal friends, relatives, or business associates.

While this latter method is the most popular way of making insurance sales, it does *not* necessarily result in the best situation for the insurance consumer. At times, the power of a referral is so strong that the buyer asks very few important questions, such as what the experience and qualifications of the person selling insurance policies might be (refer to the section, "Some questions you should ask a prospective insurance agent," found in Chapter 9, How to Get the Best Insurance Deal).

Insurance Company Incentives

A variety of incentives are frequently used by companies to generate activity (new business production) on the part of their agency sales force. Captive insurance companies appeal to their agents' desire for money and prestige (i.e., publishing their names in company-wide newsletters or making it to a top-tier "President's Club"), as well as continued employment. Independent insurance companies offer exotic trips (e.g., cruises, trips to Switzerland and Hong Kong, etc.) and additional commissions (over and above "contingent commissions" discussed earlier and in more detail below) for selling their products instead of a competitor's product. All these incentives can adversely impact the type and amount of insurance you are sold, especially if you are unaware of them.

The issue of "contingent commissions" has been touched upon earlier. However, it merits further discussion here. Remember, contingent commissions are additional commission dollars that are paid to agencies when certain, contractually agreed-upon criteria are met. While formulas for contingent commissions vary among companies and their insurance agents and brokers, some examples of when contingent commissions might be paid include:

- X amount of new business production is written with an insurance company;
- X percentage of profitability on the book of business that exists with the insurance company (usually determined by the *loss ratio* performance of the book of business); or
- A combination of these, or other stipulated criteria.

These incentives are rarely, if ever, shared with the purchaser of insurance policies. In some ways, contingent commissions are no different than bonuses paid in a variety of other industries based upon certain criteria stated in the contract between, for instance, a mortgage broker and the financial companies they represent, or a manufacturer and their manufacturer's representative, for certain agreed-upon performance objectives.

However, there clearly is the possibility that an insurance agent is writing your insurance policy with an insurance company just to earn a better sales commission bonus—rather than because that insurance carrier is the best one for you to be written with. Try to determine whether your agent is placing you with an insurance company to better their own self-interest by specifically asking whether the agent will be receiving additional compensation for selling a particular insurance policy to you. If so, ask whether the quote they are presenting is the best coverage and pricing for you, excluding the fact that the agent may be earning a contingent commission on the policy if you purchase it.

People who sell insurance must be licensed in the state where they are domiciled, and must obtain "non-resident" insurance licenses in states where they sell insurance but do not reside there. And while each state has its own laws and rules related to obtaining and maintaining insurance licenses, most initially require pre-licensing courses followed by continuing education courses. Some states, like Wisconsin, require ethics courses be taken to maintain insurance licenses.

In several of the ethics courses that I have taken, the topic of justification has been discussed. Justification can involve giving a good reason for doing (or not doing) something, but it can also be a false excuse that a person tells himself or herself as to why they do something that would not be deemed just by other people in the same circumstance based on similar facts. It is this false excuse that insurance buyers need to be wary of.

Another situation that merits discussion is when an insurance agent is so focused on receiving a contingent payment from an insurance company that he or she will refuse to write insurance policies for some customers. For example, one of my clients manufactured agricultural machinery. Since I have a duty to act in my client's best interest, one step in my annual insurance policy renewal process involves obtaining quotes to ascertain which insurance company can provide the best combination of coverages and pricing for the upcoming year.

I began my project by lining up the best insurance companies to insure my client, keeping in mind their specific business operations. One of the insurance companies appeared to be an excellent fit for my client's business.

In fact, several agents wanted this particular insurer assigned to them. I vetted each of the agents and decided to assign the insurer to the insurance agent who had the second-largest written premium with the insurance company in the state of Wisconsin. My intent was to have this agent leverage their carrier relationship to provide a very attractive quote to my client.

Towards the end of the project, just prior to the deadline given for insurance proposals, the agent who was assigned the preferred insurer told me that he did not want the insurance company to release a quote. Why? Due to the higher probability in his mind of my client having a claim based on their operations, he said he was afraid that if they had a claim after he wrote the insurance policy that this would adversely impact the amount of contingency income that he had been receiving from the insurance carrier he quoted.

While this outcome surprised me, remember that the insurance agent is an independent businessperson and is allowed to make decisions that he or she feel are in the best interest of their insurance agency. This includes areas such as profitability and which business customers they wish to insure. In my opinion, the significantly better course of action in this situation would have been for this insurance agent to decline to even get involved in the quote process for my client. If that had happened, another insurance agent would have had the opportunity to write my client's insurance with the very same insurance company.

Insurance Agent Duties

Before leaving the area of insurance sales, it is worthwhile to note that in most states insurance agents legally owe minimal duties and responsibilities to their customers. And, while many agents do not like the label "order taker," this is an accurate description of many insurance agents. Generally, it is the duty of *buyers* of insurance to tell their insurance agent the **coverage** that they desire, as well as the **limit** of insurance that they want.

Insurance *sellers* (agents) are responsible for making certain that what the customer ordered was delivered by the insurance company (known as procuring the policy), and if they cannot obtain the insurance policy requested by their client, they must let the client know this is in a timely manner. Often, little else is required of insurance agents.

However, insurance agent duties can become broader depending on a specific situation, such as when an insurance agent actively provides advice in a consultant-type role, when fees are received in addition to commissions, the length of time that the insurance customer and insurance agent relationship has been in existence, and so forth. These criteria often vary from state to state, and are sometimes referred to as a "special relationship" between the agent and their client.

Many people are surprised by the limited legal duties imposed upon insurance agents. While at first blush this may not seem fair, you must understand that there are many opportunities for misunderstandings to arise during the insurance placement process. It is not at all uncommon for insurance purchasers to say (or to think that they have said) to their insurance agent, "I want coverage for everything." Of course, this is an impossible request for an agent to meet.

Insurance Purchaser Duties

While mentioned earlier, this point cannot be overemphasized: while insurance agents have duties to their customers, insurance buyers also have duties. One important duty is to read the policies that they receive.

This does not mean that individuals and businesses that purchase insurance must know what all the policy language means, but at a minimum purchasers should review their "declarations pages," which are found at the beginning of each policy and contain a summary of information such as:

- Effective dates.
- Limits of insurance.
- Locations insured.
- Items insured (buildings, personal property, automobiles, and so forth).
- Coverages provided (major types of coverages discussed).

- Exclusions and limitations (major exclusions and limitations discussed).

- Prices that were agreed upon.

I was approached by an attorney to serve as an expert in a case he was litigating. The situation involved a married couple who had purchased a motorcycle three years prior to an accident occurring, and the injuries were substantial. When the accident occurred, it was discovered that the motorcycle had never been added to their insurance policy.

The husband and wife that had purchased the motorcycle said that they had asked their insurance agent to add the motorcycle and that he had agreed to do so. They had no written documentation (no handwritten notes or emails) related to their interaction with their insurance agent, and the insurance agent's position was that the couple had never asked him to bind coverages.

I declined to get involved in this case. Why? Because I did not feel that the plaintiffs had a case. They had no written documentation pertaining to the situation. They did not review their policy declarations pages; if they had, they would have seen that the motorcycle was not listed as an insured item. And, they should have been aware that there was no premium charge for the motorcycle. The cost for their insurance policy had remained the same.

My advice to insurance purchasers is to have their insurance agents acknowledge **in writing** any coverage that they feel is important, and to take the time to very carefully review any insurance applications prior to signing them. Ask questions if you are unclear about anything that pertains to the insurance policy you are purchasing. No one looks out for your best interests like you do.

And remember that there should be no rush to buy an insurance policy on the spot. You may wish to take the application home to review it, research areas on the application that are foreign to you, and to ask other knowledgeable persons for their input in a specific area. For instance, if you have not purchased a certain type of insurance previously, e.g., buying insurance to cover your first home purchase, perhaps you want to talk to your parents or someone else who has been through the insurance application process before. Afterwards, you can discuss their opinions with your insurance agent prior to signing the application for insurance.

More information concerning the purchase of insurance policies is found in Chapter 8, "Pricing."

Claims

An insurance policy is nothing more (or less) than a contract. Here, the contract is a promise by the insurance company to pay money if an "event" occurs that is covered under the terms of the contract. Claims adjusters are the ones who interpret whether a claim that is presented is an event that is covered under the policy (contract) purchased.

The claims department consists of adjusters who may work strictly inside, or who may work strictly outside (in the field), or a combination of the two. Simply put, adjusters are the people who control the insurance company's checkbook. Theirs is a difficult job because their company may criticize them for paying too much money on a claim, while the policyholders may criticize them for not paying enough!

Know this: Claims adjusters often have leeway when deciding how much money a policyholder or a claimant will ultimately be paid. From an insurance company standpoint, adjusters who excel in their positions are the ones who get claims closed in a reasonable time frame while paying the least amount of the insurance company's money. Additional kudos are earned by keeping customers happy, but this may be a secondary consideration.

An adjuster may, albeit infrequently, consult with an underwriter (refer to the Underwriting section for additional information about this position) for their "intent" concerning a specific insurance policy coverage provision, since underwriters are charged with coverage interpretation and are sometimes involved with drafting specific policy language. However, the ultimate decision whether to pay a claim lies with the adjuster.

Most insurance companies follow the ISO (Insurance Services Office), which promulgates the vast majority of insurance policy coverage language used by insurance companies today. Because of the wide use of this common insurance policy language, many insurance policy provisions are "court tested" and, as a result, case law exists for many coverage disputes.

Resources Used by Adjusters

Adjusters use case law, internal insurance company claims handling guidelines, and other reference/resource materials when adjusting claims.

Adjusters become aware of case law from sources including insurance company claims management, internal and external attorneys, and claims-focused magazines and periodicals. Reference materials that may be used by adjusters include items such as Fire, Casualty and Surety (FC&S) Bulletins; Insurance Services Office (ISO) ISOnet; National Council on Compensation Insurance (NCCI); the International Risk Management Institute (IRMI); the National Underwriter; Rough Notes; the National Alliance for Insurance Education and Research; A.M. Best; and a variety of other resources.

Adjuster Duties Owed to Policyholders

Insurance company adjusters have specific duties that are owed to their company's policyholders. Many of these duties are contained in the NAIC (National Association of Insurance Commissioners) Unfair Claims Settlement Practices Act model language. Provisions of this Act have been adopted as claims handling standards in legislation passed by several states.

The Unfair Claims Settlement Practices provisions provide standards that insurance companies should follow so that their insureds are treated fairly. The Act attempts to encourage insurance companies to handle claims promptly and to provide fair and equitable settlements between insurance companies and their claimants. Insurance company claims departments take the Unfair Claims Settlement Practices Act seriously.

Examples of provisions that are contained in the Unfair Claims Settlement Practices Act Model include:

- Insurance companies must fully disclose all benefits and coverages in their customer's insurance policy.

- Insurance companies cannot misrepresent their policies.

- Insurance companies cannot deny a claim based on arbitrary time limits given to customers to prove their loss or property damage.

- Insurance companies must acknowledge claims "promptly" after the claim is filed. Note that individual states may define the word "promptly" in different ways, or not at all.

- Insurance companies must provide reasonable assistance during the claims process. This includes promptly supplying customers with appropriate forms and clear instructions.

- All claim investigations must take place in a reasonable amount of time.

- Insurance companies should not enter settlement negotiations with a claimant who is not represented by an attorney or who is not an attorney.

- Insurance companies cannot send a settlement to a claimant that is less than the total cost of damages unless the customer agrees.

- Insurance companies cannot force customers to travel an unreasonable distance during their claims process; and

- If an insurance company denies or delays a claim, they must give their customer a reasonable explanation.

While many events are black and white concerning whether the policy should respond to a given claim, there are can be gray areas where a company may elect to deny payment rather than to pay a claim–and this decision is monetarily in their best interest. As stated earlier, in such situations, claims adjusters might question other internal company resources such as underwriters, or employees in the policy development department if the policy language is not clearly stated in the policy.

If the policy language is ambiguous, the policyholder should generally prevail if the disagreement moves into the court system. This is because courts view the insurance contract as strictly enforceable because the insurance policy is a "unilateral" document (drafted by only one party–the insurance company) in which the policyholder has no input in the development of the contract (this is also known as a "contract of adhesion"). As a result, ambiguities are generally decided in favor of the insurance consumer.

However, the problem ultimately becomes how long and how hard does a policyholder want to fight about coverage issues? Often, they give up too soon or forego use of an attorney, consultant, or a public adjuster, whereas the attorney, consultant or public adjuster may be able to help resolve a claim in the policyholder's favor for an additional fee.

Ambiguous Policy Wording Example

An example from my own insurance company experience will drive this point home. One of the companies I worked for (which has since been purchased by another insurance company) offered a coverage called voluntary property damage, which was often purchased by contractors (landscape gardeners, carpenters, plumbers, electricians, etc.). The intent of the coverage endorsement was to delete an exclusion in the general liability portion of the insurance policy that pertained to property in the policyholder's care, custody, or control.

For instance, if a business is involved with painting and one of the workers goes inside your house to paint a room, the entire room he will be painting is deemed to be in his care, custody, or control. If he happens to poke a hole in the wall with his ladder, the hole in the wall is something that will *not* be covered by the painting contractor's unendorsed insurance policy. The voluntary property damage endorsement was meant to override the policy exclusion to provide coverage for this type of situation.

However, the way my prior employer worded their endorsement, intended coverages were not actually provided by the endorsement in a great number of care, custody, or control claims situations. While there was not a huge premium charge for the endorsement, it was sold for many years without technically providing coverage for several claims related to care, custody, or control—which, again, was why the endorsement was developed to begin with.

It would have been relatively easy to add the intended additional coverage by clarification of policy language, but this was never done. Why not? Due to the small premium charge, it was not worth the insurance company's time and effort to correct the problem. It would have taken considerable time for the people from the information technology department to reprogram the software, time for people from the policy development department to recommend new wording, time to refile the policy wording with the Department of Insurance, time to provide updates and training to the underwriting and claims departments advising of the new wording, and so forth. Clearly, this decision was not in the best interest of the policyholder, but it was deemed a good business decision by insurance company management based purely on a "cost" basis associated with this change.

Why Claims Settlements Can Be Difficult to Understand

Consumers remain confused about the insurance claims process for many different reasons. One reason is that a claim involves understanding policy language and things such as coverage provisions, limitations, and exclusions. Another reason for consumer confusion is a lack of information about the process itself, due to a great amount of misinformation that has been spread by friends, relatives, neighbors, and others relating to insurance claims.

Common types of property claims include hail, wind, lightning, water, and theft. And, while not frequent, fire is still one of the most catastrophic types of property claims that occur.

Other events that may result in significant claims include personal liability claims, at-fault automobile accidents, on-premises medical injuries, and other types of situations where policyholders are deemed legally liable ("negligent") in some manner. It is interesting to note that according to industry statistics for homeowners' insurance claims, property damage and theft claims have accounted for nearly 80% of all claims payments, while liability claims account for less than 10% of claims paid by insurance companies.

Understand that there are few hard and fast rules when it comes to claims. There are several reasons for this. First, each claim must stand on its own merits. The facts surrounding each claim are all-important. For example, consider a hailstorm that occurs. Two next-door neighbors turn claims in to their respective insurance companies. One day soon after the storm hit, the two neighbors were talking and discover that one of them got a claim check from their insurer for $10,000 to replace his roof while the other received no payment at all.

When further facts were gathered it was discovered that the neighbor who received a claim payment had a 25-year-old roof, and the other had his roof replaced just last year. This single fact highlights a logical explanation for this claims handling discrepancy: old roofs are easily damaged, while new roofs are very resilient against hail. Thus, each of these two claims was handled properly.

Second, there is some flexibility among insurance companies relating to policy underwriting. One company may file their automobile insurance program with a rule that "forgives" the policyholder's first at-fault automobile physical damage claim if the policyholder has been insured continuously for five or more years. Another company may not have filed this same rule and, instead, surcharges for any at-fault accident.

Third, there are gray areas in the insurance policy. It is impossible for insurance policies to contemplate every single claim situation that might ever arise. Do you have a hard time believing this? As an expert witness who has provided testimony in court for insurance-related cases, I assure you this is true. Courts are constantly addressing insurance policy coverage questions.

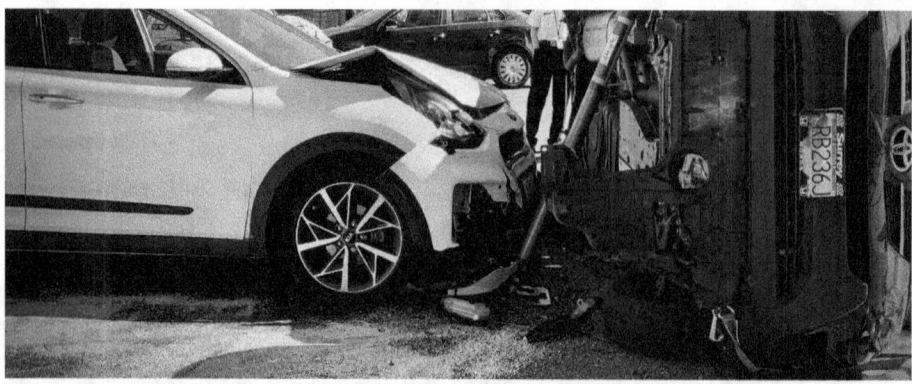

Questions and Answers Related to Payment of Claims

Individuals and businesses have many questions related to claims payments. Some of the questions that I have been asked during my consulting projects include:

- Will my policy be cancelled if I turn in a claim?
- Will my personal insurance rates increase if I make a claim?
- Am I better off paying small claims out of pocket, or should I turn in every possible claim to my insurance company?
- Are claims that I make under my business insurance policy viewed in the same way as claims I make under my personal insurance policies?
- What are my options if coverage for my claim is denied by my insurance company?
- What can I do if I do not feel that I am being treated fairly in the claims process (this may involve situations such as the length of time it is taking for a claim to be settled or the amount of money the insurance company is offering as a claim settlement total dollar value)?
- Who can I trust to give me advice about my specific claim situation?

For the reasons previously mentioned, keep in mind that there may be different outcomes in the way that adjusters will handle two similar claims. Nevertheless, here are reasonable answers to the above questions.

Will my policy be cancelled if I turn in a claim?

Maybe–depending on the type of claim, the number of claims you have made in a specified time frame and the underwriting criteria in place at your insurance company. You can ask your insurance agent what impact making a claim will have, but know this: insurance agents are required to inform insurance companies about what you tell them. Therefore, it is possible that your claim situation may be held against you even if your claim is not formally turned in.

An example of this is if you had an at-fault minor fender bender and contacted your insurance agent to discuss whether you should make a claim. He or she most likely would inform the insurance company of the occurrence even if that was not your intent. Why? Because policyholders have a duty to make claims as soon as practicable. If a claim is not made and the minor fender bender turns ugly–for instance, the other party decides they have whiplash in addition to car damages–insureds face the possibility of a claims denial because you did not let the insurance company investigate in a timely manner.

While you may not realize it, insurers are interested in any significant changes that occur in the risks they are accepting. In insurance company terminology this is known as a "material change in risk." So, if you had no dangerous breed of dog when you first purchased your homeowner's policy, the insurance company expects that will remain the case throughout the time that they provide your insurance. But if you buy a dangerous dog (e.g., a Rottweiler, Pit Bull, Akita), this presents a different set of circumstances from the standpoint that the dog could cause damage by destroying property or injuring someone else by scratching, biting, or attacking them.

Generally, the owner of a dog is held liable for damages or injury the dog causes, and the specific breeds mentioned above are more prone to cause injuries than other breeds. The worst scenarios involve children under seven years of age. When a child is younger than seven, courts may feel they have not reached the "age of reason," and since their judgment is not yet formed, they cannot be held liable for their actions, including things such as teasing a dog. If the child is not liable, *you* are. If you are liable for injuries, your insurance company may step in to pay damages you owe. But, if they did not know you have a dog, especially a dangerous breed of dog, they will not look favorably upon paying a claim involving a dog.

It is important to know that many communities have ordinances and laws that pertain to dog ownership. These deal with things such as mandatory leash laws and dog bites. Claims adjusters take these laws into account, along with the specific claim situation details, when handling a dog bite claim. If you own a dog, I encourage you to become familiar with dog laws in your own community.

Will my personal insurance rates increase if I make a claim?

Many years ago, homeowner policies made money for insurance companies. More recently, however, this has not been the case. There have been significant weather-related claims that, while not the fault of insureds, have nevertheless resulted in claims payments. Tornados, hail, strong winds, lightning storms, hurricanes and more have given rise to millions of dollars in claims payments by insurance carriers. Therefore, your homeowner policy may now very well cost you more if you make any claim against it.

Concerning automobile policies, you are very likely to pay more (via a policy "surcharge") for any at-fault accident. In addition, your auto policy price will likely increase if a household driver receives a ticket for any type of moving violation. Statistically speaking, nearly one-third of fatal accidents involve speeding or driving too fast for conditions. If you speed, insurers have proven that any accident you have in the future will be more severe than if you do not speed. Therefore, you are charged a higher rate now for the accident that may occur in the future.

For homeowners and automobile policies, insurance companies typically take a long, hard look at the frequency of losses incurred. Since homeowners' premiums are generally less than $3,000 annually, insurance companies cannot afford to pay out many claims and hope to remain profitable. While automobile insurance rates are somewhat higher, payments for liability and medical claims can involve significant payments. Again, insurance companies cannot pay many high-dollar automobile claims for an individual policyholder and remain profitable. What about a policyholder who has several very small claims? Underwriters adhere to the following rule: *frequency breeds severity*. In other words, if a policyholder has a history of small claims, a big claim is almost certain to follow at some point in the future.

Am I better off paying small claims out of pocket or turning in each claim?

It may benefit you *not* to turn in small claims. It does, however, depend on the type of claim and the facts involved. For instance, if $520 of personal clothing is stolen out of your car, and if you carry a $500 deductible, it makes little sense to turn in the claim. However, if someone is injured from a slip and fall in front of your home on an icy sidewalk that you did not shovel for three days, you *should* turn in the claim, even if the injured person says that they will not hold you liable. This type of claim may worsen over time and turn ugly for a variety of reasons, so it is important to provide your insurance company with information concerning the situation as soon as possible, so they can investigate and hire defense counsel should the need arise.

As a reminder, if you do not turn in this type of claim, the insurance company has the right to reject payment for this very reason. This is known as prejudicing the insurance company's rights by not giving them the opportunity to become involved at the time that the accident took place.

Are claims I turn in under my business insurance policy viewed the same way as claims I make under my personal insurance policies?

No. Most business policies are underwritten on a "loss ratio" basis. This means that insurance company underwriters weigh the amount of premiums "paid in" against the amounts of claims dollars "paid out." While different companies apply different profitability criteria, most insurance companies are content with a pure loss ratio of 50% or less. However, the higher the loss ratio of your specific insurance policy, the more likely that a higher renewal price increase will be applied.

In addition to the loss ratio on a business insurance policy, underwriters review the frequency, types of losses, and dollar amounts paid for individual claims paid. If a business policy generates a significant premium but has a claim that involves a potentially serious consequence, this alone may cause a large price increase or even cancellation of the policy.

In addition, underwriters review risk characteristics and may take adverse action against a business policyholder if negative information is discovered. For instance, if a business hires a driver who has one or more DUI (driving under the influence) violations on their motor vehicle record, the insurance company will likely try to exclude the driver (where permissible by law) or may cancel the commercial automobile policy.

What are my options if coverage for my claim is denied by my insurance company?

A good first step is to discuss the situation directly with your insurance claims adjuster. Make certain they understand the facts clearly. If they have denied your claim, they should cite the specific policy language they relied upon. If you continue to feel the insurance company has wrongly denied your claim, you should next discuss your claim with your insurance agent. Your agent has a legal, dual fiduciary responsibility to act not only in the insurance company's best interest, but also in your best interest.

Keep in mind, however, your agent likely has thousands or even millions of dollars of written premiums with the insurance company compared to the relatively low premium dollars that you pay for your insurance. Therefore, agents may have an inherent bias that works in the favor of the insurance company. After all, if they lose you as a client, it may cost them insurance commissions in the amount of $1,500 or so, whereas if they lose their insurance company contract it may cost them more than $100,000 of income. Another factor may be that your insurance agent might make it a personal practice not to get involved with claims because they feel that adjusters are in the very best position to interpret claims.

Remember that payment of claims is the reason insurance companies are in business. However, they must follow their policy (contract) wording during the claims adjustment process. If they pay claims that are not covered under the insurance policy then many other facets involving their insurance policy are impacted, such as:

- Policy rates may go up since actuaries did not contemplate payment for uncovered claims.
- Courts may broaden the insurance company's liability for other claims that were never intended to be covered. This can result from a plaintiff's attorney asking the insurance company if they ever

intentionally paid claims that were not technically covered by their insurance contract.

- Claims adjusters, underwriters and the marketing department may become confused concerning coverages provided under insurance policies sold to the public.

One final comment is warranted before leaving the topic of insurance claims. Some insurance companies use only their own inside insurance adjusters; some insurance companies use mainly "independent contractor" (third-party, or outside) adjusters, and other insurance companies use a combination of inside and outside adjusters.

As a general statement, I have found that third-party adjusters do not handle claims as well as adjusters who are insurance company employees. My guess is that this is due to several factors, including lack of training, frequency of employee turnover in independent adjuster companies, and their performance is based upon a different customer base (for inside adjusters, their customer is their policyholder; for third-party adjusters, their customer is the insurance company itself). There may also be a possible lack of accountability, i.e., complaints against individual company adjusters go directly to insurance company claims supervisors, while complaints against independent adjusters may never get back to appropriate insurance carrier personnel.

Are all third-party independent adjusters bad adjusters? Certainly not. However, during my career I have often noticed differences between employee adjusters and third-party adjusters, and that the balance tips in favor of inside adjusters doing a better job overall.

Be advised that some insurance policies for large businesses list specific adjusters in their policies and these are agreed upon by both carrier and insured.

What can I do if I do not feel that I am being treated fairly in the claims process?

This may involve situations such as the length of time it is taking for a claim to be settled or the amount of money the insurance company is offering as a claim settlement total dollar value.

After discussing your situation with your insurance adjuster and your insurance agent to no avail, you may next wish to discuss your claim denial with a public adjuster, an insurance consultant, or an attorney. Also, you have the right to involve the Commissioner of Insurance in your applicable state where coverages apply by filing a complaint and asking that they review the circumstances of your claim denial. The insurance complaint is generally filed in your state of domicile, but this may change depending on the specific facts of the claim that is made.

My experience has been that there is little downside in making an insurance department complaint, and by submitting a complaint to the department of insurance, it assures that the insurance carrier will review your claim at a higher level and that they may ultimately change their prior decisions in your favor.

However, keep in mind that most insurance claims are handled efficiently and correctly by insurance company adjusters. Therefore, if your insurance claim has been denied, or if you are not paid as much as you think your claim is worth, it is quite possible that there truly is no coverage for your claim under your insurance policy, or that the value of your claim is not as high as you believe it is.

Who can I trust to give me advice about my specific claim situation?

First and foremost, you should be able to trust your claim adjuster. They have a responsibility to walk you through the claims process and to explain the insurance policy provisions that apply to your claim. But relationships between an adjuster and their insured can break down between the time that a claim is first opened and the time it is closed.

Circumstances that result in an insurance claim are often emotional situations for insureds and communication can collapse between an adjuster and their policyholder. Since insureds are unfamiliar with how the claims process works, it can be frustrating, and sometimes infuriating, to allow another party to control the claim and to make decisions that may involve little input from you. Adjusters are the ones who decide if there is coverage and, if so, how much your claim is worth.

But, claims adjusters are human and they can make mistakes. They can have bad days. They can have other things on their mind and they can be cranky from lack of sleep due to staying up with their sick two-year-old child. So, perhaps one interaction with the adjuster will go south for these types of reasons. If so, try to overlook one bad experience and focus on the next interaction.

However, there *are* some bad adjusters. Some people are not cut out for handling claims but are still employed by an insurance carrier in that capacity. When you have tried and tried again to get along with an adjuster, but cannot, it is time to take the next step, which is to speak with the adjuster's manager. Tell him or her your perspective about inadequacies you have encountered in the handling of your claim and ask for their help, including asking that your adjuster be replaced with someone else. While there is no guarantee that your adjuster will be replaced, or that any other action will be taken, this approach provides additional documentation for your file if you need to take the next step.

Consulting with an attorney is generally a good next step, and there is generally no charge for your initial consultation. However, like many other situations involving important decisions, perform your due diligence before deciding to hire an attorney.

Not long ago I received a phone call from a plaintiff's attorney at a well-known law firm that specialized in personal injury cases. She was looking for an expert to help in an insurance agent errors and omissions case she had accepted.

The case involved a situation like ones that I had been involved in several times before, but as I offered advice based on the specific facts of her case, I felt that she lacked experience in this type of circumstance. Based on what she told me, my feeling was that not only did she have a weak case against the insurance agent, but that she was also struggling with how best to proceed with an agent errors and omissions case. Some plaintiffs' attorneys accept cases on a contingency basis (payment only if they win), but some charge clients on an hourly basis. Woe to the persons who hired this attorney if she charged them hourly.

Last, it is possible to hire an insurance consultant or a public adjuster to assist with a claim. But these types of occupations are generally hired only when the claim is very large. If hired by the person who had the claim, the consultant or public adjuster can step into the shoes of the person making the claim and can interact with the insurance carrier directly. In addition, insurance consultants and public adjusters can be hired by attorneys to assist with their client's legal case against an insurance company.

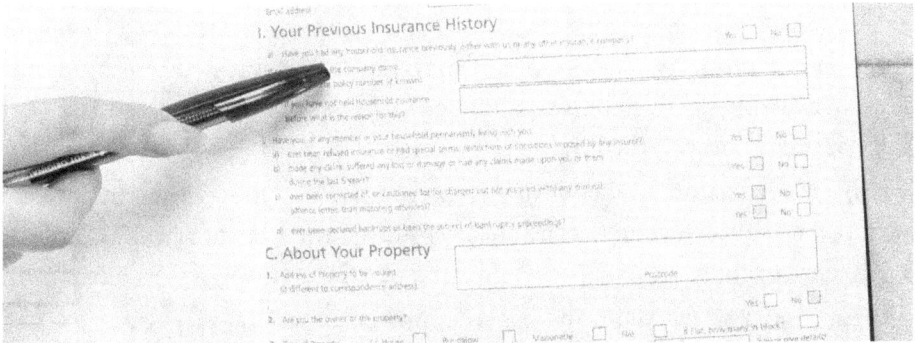

Underwriting

Underwriting is the analysis of the characteristics of a risk to decide if the risk is *acceptable, unacceptable,* or *acceptable if certain requested conditions (changes) are met.* Underwriters review applications that are submitted and decide whether the characteristics presented meet company guidelines that are in place for that specific type of business (such as homeowners, auto or businessowner policies).

Two important risk characteristics that underwriters keep in mind during their underwriting process involves the determination of whether a *moral hazard* or a *morale hazard* exists.

A moral hazard involves personal traits and characteristics that increase the probability of an insurance-related loss occurring in the future due to bad habits or morals. It may indicate an inability to distinguish from right and wrong behavior, i.e., someone who has been convicted of three driving while intoxicated (also known as driving under the influence) violations during the past three years. Insurers have a concern that these individuals have little regard for laws prohibiting such behavior, and that they may be involved in auto accidents where others are seriously injured. And they are more likely to be involved in other adverse insurance-related behaviors.

A related, but somewhat different, hazard is a morale hazard. This includes people or businesses that have a lackadaisical outlook and do not care for their property or care about hazards on their property. An example is a someone who exhibits no pride in ownership and does not maintain the property that they own. Such a person is more likely to make insurance claims for damage that might have been avoided if proper maintenance and care was given to their owned property. These types of individuals and businesses also present a higher likelihood of liability claims for insurers, due to increased trip and fall hazards to others, for instance.

By its very nature, underwriting is discriminatory. Underwriters apply a set of approved company criteria, and are often also allowed personal leeway (known as "underwriting judgment") when making decisions on specific accounts.

An underwriter typically has the power to make exceptions to the insurance company's guidelines and to issue a policy based on a submission, even though that submission does not technically qualify. If an exception is made, it is typically documented, and is frequently reviewed by management.

Underwriters also possess pricing authority. This is true in both personal lines and commercial lines, though much more evident with large commercial accounts. A frequent pricing method used in personal lines (i.e., auto and homeowner policies) is application of preferred credits, or the use of a tiered approach. Whichever method of pricing is used, the idea is that the best risks (those that the company underwriter feels will have no future claims) get the best pricing. This is not always the case, however, as favors are frequently done on the underwriting level based on things such as an underwriter's relationship with an agent.

One of the craziest things about the underwriting process is the archaic rating methodology that is used by some insurance companies to price commercial lines (business insurance) policies. While some carriers are making positive changes in this regard, others rely on arcane rating systems to get their policies issued. There is no good (quick and easy-to-use) rating system that is widely available in the insurance industry. Some insurance companies use proprietary rating systems and others purchase off-the-shelf rating software that is tweaked according to their specific needs.

A great amount of effort and time is required to rate coverages that the insurance company provides. All the customer and agent want is a bottom-line price. They do not care how difficult it is to massage the insurance company's computer software to come up with a price. Much of this problem has to do with the history of commercial lines ratemaking and the fact that there are many facets involved with coming up with a business policy's price.

As an example, for insurance companies that follow Insurance Services Office (ISO) filed rates and rules, rating a property risk involves considering things such as Basic Group I Symbols, Basic Group II Symbols, Height, Building Construction Symbol, Basic Group I Rate, Section I General Rules, Section II Coverage Form Rules, Causes of Loss Form Rules, Basic Group I Class Rates, and much, much, much more! And these apply only to Commercial Property insurance policies. Other commercial policies, such as general liability and automobile have their own unique rating methodologies.

A major overhaul of the commercial lines products rating methodologies is needed to simplify the way that accounts are priced. The result will be a welcome reduction in the amount of time it takes to issue a commercial insurance policy, as well as a better understanding by consumers of how prices are determined.

Policy Services

Policy Services provides the internal assistance necessary for the insurance company to get their policies issued. This includes rating entry, secretarial-related work, and other jobs that move a policy through the organization and out their doors.

Many insurance companies also include some type of quality control as part of their Policy Services Department. Quality control entails the review of issued policies to ascertain whether they contain the policy forms, endorsements, exclusions, and other items that match the insurance coverage requested by the consumer.

Amazingly enough, some insurance companies have completely done away with the quality control function. For example, during a deposition, I discovered that a large, national insurance company relies completely upon their insurance agents to review issued policies for accuracy. The attorney for the insurance carrier stated that the insurance company feels it is solely the responsibility of their insurance agent representatives to review policies as part of the services the agency provides to earn the commissions paid by the insurance company.

I find this stance utterly amazing. This position is like an automobile manufacturer producing a new vehicle and expecting the dealership that sells the car to perform a multi-page, in depth product safety check of the car. A cursory review makes sense, but not an engineering analysis. To me, common sense dictates that the party that has the most knowledge about the product being produced should implement quality control procedures.

Audit Department

The main purpose of the Audit Department is to find out if there have been exposure changes in a commercial policy since the last anniversary date. Many commercial insurance policies are issued on an auditable basis. This means that the initial insurance premium is based upon an estimate—a "best-guess" as to what the business exposure will be at the end of the policy term. Auditable insurance policies include General Liability, Worker's Compensation, Business Automobile, and may include certain other policies such as Commercial Inland Marine and some Non-Standard insurance policies.

Auditable policies are rated based upon estimated exposures. For example, General Liability rating may be based upon things such as square footage (area), gross sales receipts, units, payroll, admissions, or "A-Rates" where underwriting judgment is used to determine a rate to charge for the exposure. For worker's compensation, rates are based upon a worker's job duties (classifications), and payrolls are assigned to each classification on the current policy.

Here is an example of an auditable policy situation: Acme Widgets has an insurance policy that is effective January 1, 2025, and expires on January 1, 2026. Acme plans sales of $1,000,000 during the 2025 policy year. Therefore, the insurance policy is issued using a specific rate (i.e., 1.57 per $1,000 of sales), which is chosen by the underwriter. This rate is then applied to the estimated sales value.

The policy is issued with a General Liability premium of $1,570, which reflects the 1.57 rate x 1,000 exposure units ($1,000,000 dollars of sales). The policy is audited six months after the end of the policy term (June 30,

2026) and it is discovered that Acme had actually sold $2,000,000 worth of widgets during the policy period.

In this case, an additional premium is developed taking the 1.57 specific rate and multiplying it by 1,000 additional sales exposure units (representing the additional $1,000,000 of sales that took place during 2025). Another $1,570 of premium is owed to the insurance company because of the actual sales that took place at Acme Widgets.

This is fair to all parties because additional sales represent additional exposure to risk for the insurance company and they are entitled to additional premium to offset the additional risks present. Alternately, if only $500,000 in sales were generated by Acme during 2025, they would be entitled to a credit of $785 for their reduced exposure basis. If a credit is due to the policyholder, a check is issued by the insurance company and sent to the policyholder.

Note that there are some insurance policies that are issued on a non-auditable basis. Generally, this is a positive situation for the insurance customer because it allows businesses to better budget their annual insurance costs, and it can result in cost-savings for businesses that are growing. However, for those businesses with declining sales, an auditable policy is best since they will likely get money refunded after an audit takes place once the policy period ends.

Loss Control

Loss Control (also known as Loss Control Engineering or Safety Engineering) is a service offered by insurance companies to clients who meet certain criteria.

These criteria include the class (type) of business (a large manufacturing business certainly warrants loss control while a small ice cream store generally does not); premiums generated by the account (many insurance companies do not feel it is cost effective to offer these types of services to an account that generates less than $25,000 or so of annual insurance premium); and on a case-by-case basis (usually the result of a customer or agent request).

Loss control is a valuable service if the individual performing the inspection is well-trained and experienced in looking at the specific type of business you own. Where this potential benefit fails is when the loss control inspector is not knowledgeable, or when business owners do not follow through on specific key recommendations generated during the personal inspection of their business.

Why is controlling losses a worthy endeavor? Applying risk management techniques is a prudent behavior because having a claim is seldom a good thing. Even though the insurance company may pay you for a covered loss, there are ancillary costs that are not covered. Many things suck up your time during a claim, such as paperwork associated with making the claim, the time it takes to prove the claim and damages related to the claim—if an insurer does not issue a check for full damages for your claim. And there is also a great deal of unreimbursed time involved in efforts to sue your insurance company, if you go in that direction.

In addition, loss control reports are usually sent to underwriters as part of the underwriting process, either before a policy is written or afterwards. If positive information is contained in the report, underwriters can incentivize businesses with things such as premium savings or better deductibles. Alternatively, if the loss control information is negative, underwriting can decide not to write a policy, or can offer higher prices, higher deductibles, lower limits, more exclusions, and so forth.

So, a positive focus on loss control is a good thing from both a personal and business standpoint. To further drive this point home, here is an illustration of the positive impact of initiating loss control measures for a coffee manufacturer or coffee roaster.

Coffee dust causes problems for both employees and the building where the coffee is roasted. It can accumulate in machines that roast coffee, as well as in ductwork. And, if not cleaned regularly, a fire can result that potentially damages both the building and contents. In addition, during the coffee roasting production process, employees can inhale coffee dust. Coffee dust contains gasses, vapors, and other lung and eye irritants, resulting in in coughing, shortness of breath and more.

Addressing and preventing potential building and employee issues is wholeheartedly better than dealing with the aftermath of problems that arise after such damage occurs. Thus, it is worthwhile to spend time and money on loss prevention up front.

Loss control can work miracles in bringing down both the frequency and severity of worker's compensation injuries. Loss control engineers can help implement safety programs, and they work with human resources, as well as supervisors and foremen, to ensure the success of safety programs. They can also address things such as potential products liability claims and whether the business is complying with current work-related laws and regulations (i.e., OSHA). However, one of the most important things that loss control engineers can do is to get owners or top-level managers involved in key loss control issues. If top management is not 100% behind recommended changes, necessary loss control changes–and resulting business improvements–will simply not occur.

Never underestimate the importance of good company management. I have worked with companies that have had a mentality of "good enough," and those that were unwilling to instill sound operating practices because of "hassle factors," including costs, involved with making changes. Insurance companies seldom desire to insure this type of company. On the other hand, I have seen a change of management come with a corresponding change of operational mentality. New management enacted new policies, procedures, and safety requirements–and the difference was amazing. Where old management was content with no changes, new management abhorred claims and their company became much more profitable as a result. This increased profitability resulted in part from reduced insurance premiums due to improved claims results. Same company name but a completely different managerial mindset.

For effective loss control, the insurance company representative should visit the business a minimum of twice per year. Four times to twelve times per year may be necessary initially for businesses that have multiple exposures, or ones that have high risk exposures–such as manufacturers of automobile parts. The frequency depends upon the type of business, the focus of the loss control initiatives (i.e., worker's compensation vs. premises liability related) and/or the severity of problems that are discovered. But more than likely, the insurance company will not proactively offer a high number of visits without its customer demanding it.

Just because a company does not qualify for insurance carrier loss control services does not mean that loss control should be ignored. Alternative sources of loss control services and information are available if a business does not meet the insurance company's minimum loss control qualifications. These include hiring private loss control engineering firms, requesting an Occupational Safety and Health Administration (OSHA) inspection, or using other state or local government agencies.

Smaller businesses can also request a no-cost, confidential OSHA consultation that focuses on finding and fixing workplace hazards. This focus on finding and fixing hazards is separate from OSHA enforcement and the services are generally provided by state agencies or universities. For additional information visit https://www.osha.gov/consultation.

Other resources may be available, depending on the state in which a business is located. For example, in the state of Wisconsin, a worker's compensation classification code audit can be provided by an entity known as the Wisconsin Compensation Rating Bureau (WCRB). During their inspection, they will also point out safety concerns that they might observe.

4.

Other Insurance Company Support Positions

There are other positions at insurance companies that operate behind the scenes and can impact how you are treated as an insurance company policyholder. These positions support the infrastructure of insurance companies and can include *Legal, Actuary, Subrogation, Internal Audit, Product Development, Information Technology* and *Management*.

Legal

The legal department usually supports the claims department. It ultimately decides which claims should be fought (company position defended), which outside attorneys (independent, stand-alone law firms that represent insurance companies and their insureds) will be used in litigation support matters, and at what point a settlement should be considered. In my experience, most "internal" attorneys do not possess the same depth of legal courtroom expertise as those attorneys who practice law as a part of a law firm. Thus, outside attorneys usually represent the concerns of the insurance company in court.

Company attorneys may also provide support to human resources and other internal departments in areas such as setting guidelines and policies, as well as providing guidance on internal employee claims and suits, such as worker's compensation claims and employment practices liability suits for things such as age discrimination.

An ancillary reason that outside attorneys are used by insurance companies is to avoid possible conflict of interest claims by their insureds. If an insurance company uses its own attorneys to represent its insureds, it may be accused of acting in its own best interest–i.e., by trying to pay as little as possible for a claim, regardless of the merits.

An example of this is where an insurance company's insured is sued due to the negligent operation of a motor vehicle. If the injuries are substantial and the policy liability limits are low, the insurance company may not want to spend money on defense of their insured and might simply offer policy limits. However, this approach can expose the policyholder's personal assets. Courts have decided that the duty to defend an insured is as important, if not more important, than the duty to pay for damages. Insurance companies may be able to "pay and walk," but must be very careful in these situations. Refer to Chapter 7, Insurance Litigation, for additional information.

Another reason to use outside law firms is because of the wide variety of subject-matter expertise offered by external law firms. It is difficult for lawyers to be experts in all areas of law, thus, if expertise is required in special areas such as products liability, product recall, pollution, and so forth, attorneys are sought out who possess this specific expertise. Also, external attorneys have more experience in preparing for and presenting the insurance company's position before a judge, should a case move to trial.

Actuary

"Kill the actuaries" is the battle-cry of many underwriters and marketing representatives. The purpose of those in the actuarial department is to statistically analyze the rate structure of insurance policies by line of business (i.e., commercial property, commercial general liability, commercial automobile, homeowners, and personal automobile) to decide whether a rate increase or decrease is needed, and if so, by how much.

Ratemaking can be a matter of massaging the numbers to say what you want them to say. For example, actuarial data for an insurance company's State of Wisconsin homeowners' policies (referred to as "book of business") may call for an overall increase of 10 percent based upon statistics gathered by their actuarial department. This rate increase may be based on a review of the company's income and expenses, where total premiums (income) received is compared to the company's expenses. Insurance company expenses include claims paid, outstanding liabilities (known as "incurred but not reported," or "IBNR" within the industry) and other company expenses such as payroll, benefits, overhead and profit.

This 10 percent rate increase recommended by Actuarial is then reviewed by Marketing and/or Underwriting (depending on where the responsibility for this task falls). Joint discussions are then held between these departments and senior management to determine the ultimate policy price increase that will be taken. Discussions may include areas such as statutory rate adequacy, marketing competitiveness, and future income and expense projections (including regulatory impact, time value of money, and so on).

Rate discussions are always a balancing act. The insurance company must charge enough money to stay solvent but cannot charge too much compared to its competition. If pricing gets too far above competitor pricing, the insurance company is likely to not only shut down new business income, but also faces the loss of existing business they have written. The result is that profitability may suffer even more.

An additional factor that insurance companies must keep in mind is that their best customers may leave (i.e., automobile policyholders with good credit ratings, good driving records and claims-free) if prices are raised too much. The remaining customers might be those who are less desirable because they may not qualify for an insurance policy at another carrier. Thus, remaining insureds may be involved in more accidents and will be less profitable for the insurer, further deteriorating the insurance company's bottom line.

My experience has been that a great deal of emphasis is placed upon marketing competitiveness during actuarial discussions. The marketing department often plays a lead role in discussions and is typically successful in convincing senior management that although actuarial data may call for a 10 percent statewide increase, a lower percentage of increase should be implemented due to marketplace competitiveness.

The Real Scoop on Actuarial Changes

Understand that the above example is quite simplified. In reality, much fine-tuning takes place during the ratemaking process. For instance, rates in one territory with poor loss experience may be supported (offset) by another territory with good experience.

This means that, rather than taking a 10 percent statewide homeowners rate increase, insurance companies segment rate information using a multitude of factors. Using homeowners as an example, some of the factors considered include the age of the home, its value, the geographical territory, liability values, protection class, and much more. As a result of this ratemaking process, the insurance company's homeowner rates may ultimately decrease for homes located in Milwaukee, Wisconsin, but this will be offset by taking a 20 percent increase for homes insured in Superior, Wisconsin. Therefore, the desired net effect of a 10 percent overall increase for the entire insurance company is achieved.

Once new rates are agreed upon, the company files its rates with the Department of Insurance in the state(s) where the new rates will be in effect. Where a *file-and-use* law is in effect, the insurance company must submit its new rates before they become effective. Actual approval is *not* required before the rates are used. However, the Department of Insurance can disapprove the rates if they find them in violation of any statutes. To play it safe, insurers often wait until after the Department of Insurance has reviewed and approved their rates just to make sure that their company will not need to recall their new rates after they have been published and distributed to their agency sales force.

If a *prior-approval* law is in effect, all rates must be filed with the state's Department of Insurance (Insurance Commissioner's office) prior to use and must be formally approved or disapproved.

It cannot be overemphasized that the setting of rates presents a difficult dichotomy for insurance companies. Regardless of what the mathematical models may say, the insurance company must compete in the real world against other companies trying to sell similar products. If an actuary suggests a rate increase of 20 percent and this puts the insurance company's pricing structure at a total of 15 percent over marketplace competitors, very little additional new business is likely to be written. On the other hand, by completely ignoring the actuary's findings, the company is jeopardizing its surplus (the funds available for paying future claims) and might be placed under a state's Insurance Commissioner watch as a result.

Subrogation

The subrogation clause contained in property and liability policies give insurers the right to take legal action against third parties who are responsible for a loss to an insured for which a claim has been paid. If, for instance, an automobile accident occurs where someone other than you (the policyholder) is clearly at fault in damaging your car, or injuring you or other occupants in your car, your insurance company may directly pay you for damages, bodily injuries, or medical payments, and then subrogate against the at-fault party.

Since the legal system holds individuals responsible for damages that result from their negligence, the at-fault party must pay to make the innocent party whole. When your insurance company makes payment to you, they are then entitled to "step into your shoes" to recover payments from the negligent party who was responsible for your accident.

Subrogation department personnel, often referred to as Subrogation Specialists, are known as the "bad boys" of the insurance company. They typically work as a part of the claims department and chase down individuals or companies that owe money to the insurance company.

Steps in the Subrogation Process

The first step in the subrogation process is to determine whether the at-fault party has insurance. Using automobile insurance as an example, most drivers on the road today carry auto insurance, but there are still many people who do not.

The easiest way to determine whether an insurance policy is in effect is to send a letter directly to the person who caused the accident. The letter will state that evidence shows they are personally responsible for all damages to an innocent party; however, if they provide their insurance company information, their insurance company will be dealt with directly instead.

Next, if the at-fault party has insurance, the subrogation specialist will contact that insurance company directly to demand that they reimburse his or her carrier for all damages incurred. If they refuse, negotiations about the amount owed may take place if, for instance, the facts do not prove the other party was 100 percent at fault. Or, the situation may be referred to the insurance company's attorney to determine whether a lawsuit should be filed to obtain compensation.

If the negligent party does not have insurance, he or she will personally owe the amount of damages for the repair of the policyholder's banged-up vehicle, as well as for other damages, such as medical and bodily injury payments, and must ultimately pay any outstanding legal judgment on an out-of-pocket basis. Payment plans, including garnishment of wages, may be set up for repayment of what is owed.

As someone who has had direct responsibility for subrogation during my insurance career, I can attest that people are generally uncooperative when it comes to admitting their fault and in sharing their insurance company information. It is not at all uncommon to send three or more requests for information.

Heightened Insurance Carrier Focus on Subrogation

More and more insurance companies are focused on subrogation. Why is this? Because of the potential to recoup dollars paid out to policyholders. Sometimes *big* dollars. Subrogation efforts can amount to thousands or even hundreds of thousands of dollars. However, even small dollar amounts can add up to significant dollar amounts for insurance companies.

In addition, insurance companies are becoming more aggressive in pursuing certain specific types of subrogation. For instance, companies are recognizing the potential that worker's compensation subrogation holds.

Insurance companies must pay work comp claims according to state statutes that generally demand payment on a "no-fault" basis. In other words, if an employee is injured due to a work-related occurrence, insurance companies must make payment to the employee for the incurred injury regardless of fault.

However, it is possible that the injury was the result of the negligence of a third-party (unrelated to the employer). In this situation, the insurance company is entitled to demand payment from the at-fault third-party. If the negligent party does not agree to make payment based upon the demand letter, the insurance company that made payment is legally entitled to bring a lawsuit against the negligent party.

Many times, outside collection agencies or attorneys are used for subrogation purposes where the potential of a large dollar recovery amount exists. Understand that these people often play hardball! In some of these types of outsourced subrogation situations, the subrogation firms are paid based upon a percentage of the total dollar recovery amount. As a result, they are aggressive not only in their attempts to receive payment, but also related to the dollar amounts sought.

Internal Audit

The internal audit department reviews internal insurance company underwriting, claims, and other department activities to make sure the various departments within the insurance company are acting within company and legal guidelines. In addition, management frequently requests that a certain underwriting line of business, or a particular type of claim adjuster file (i.e., liability adjuster), be reviewed to see if there are areas for possible improvement.

Another reason for internal review of underwriting and claims files is to discover whether any wrongdoing (i.e., fraud) has occurred. Auditors look for both isolated situations as well as for patterns of negative activities that have occurred. Auditors review files, note observations, and make recommendations for change in the hopes of seeing improvements in the very near future.

Internal audit also monitors things such as possible vendor (or agent, etc.) kickbacks to employees or expense report accuracy, and they ascertain whether employees are doing their jobs honestly. I have known of situations where claims adjusters invented a dummy corporation and then began making claims payments to their dummy corporation for building repairs–while pocketing all the money.

I have also seen situations where agents take money from clients but keep the money and pay their clients' claims out of their own private bank accounts. Here, insurance policies were never actually issued and the insurance company was unaware that the person had purchased insurance. Never heard of such a thing? It is no surprise since insurance companies rarely, if ever, want this type of fraud publicized since it gives them very bad press and makes their other policyholders nervous.

Product Development

When it comes to product development, insurance companies are a strange lot. They tout their differences and state reasons why they are better than their competitors. However, insurance companies often sell very similar products at similar prices whether they are selling homeowners, automobile or businessowners policies. One of the reasons for this is that insurance companies frequently use the same rates and coverage language as their basis of coverage–items that are provided by the Insurance Services Office (ISO) or by the American Association of Insurance Services (AAIS).

Since the insurance policy is a contract, insurers are comfortable using contract language that has been "court tested." While prior lawsuits provide valuable case law for insurance carriers, it also ties their hands when it comes to offering innovative products in the marketplace. The result is that insurance companies many times sell very similar "black boxes."

While customers might want a black-and-white box, the company says all it can offer is a black box, take it or leave it. This can leave their customer unsatisfied, which results in them looking for alternate ways to get what they want from an insurance coverage standpoint.

Most carriers keep close tabs on what their competitors are up to. If a new product is introduced by the competition, other companies typically wait for six months or so to see how well the product has been received in the marketplace. If the new product has generated decent revenues, while incurring limited claims payments, other companies may introduce their own "similar" new product following what the trend-setting company had introduced.

Everyone at insurance companies keeps their eyes and ears open concerning their competition, but typically it is the marketing department that feeds competitive information back to their own insurance company's management. Once the information is received, the marketing department makes suggestions for change, if they feel it makes sense. Senior management from both claims and underwriting then either agree or disagree with the recommendation(s). If consensus is reached within the insurance company departments, the product idea moves forward through the product development team, and a new product is born. The proposed product is then reviewed by other departments, such as the legal and information technology departments, prior to release.

Since some of the items developed are new to a company, there may be some ambiguity concerning exactly what coverages are intended to be provided. As a result, there can be a lengthy amount of time after a new product's introduction to allow the claims department to have internal discussions concerning whether certain claims that have been made should or should not be paid by the insurance company.

Information Technology

Programming of new products by the information technology department (IT) is an extremely important part of the introduction of new insurance company products. In fact, this single department can cause a new product to be put on hold for a short time, a long time, or even indefinitely. Therefore, insurance companies habitually start their new product development process by having discussions with the IT department to make certain that they have the capacity to provide programming support for the introduction of a new product.

Keep in mind that insurance policies are essentially issued as the result of software programming. Policy language, attachments (known as "endorsements") and rating to achieve a price all result from software programming. Some insurance companies develop all their own forms, which requires a large investment in IT programming dollars. Other companies purchase parts of their policy formatting or rating programs from third parties. But no matter what approach is taken by insurance companies, the IT department plays a key role in their organization. There is always some kind of work for them to do.

The IT department at insurance companies operates in much the same way as the assembly line at a car manufacturer. This is the guts of the production process and this is the department that can bottleneck the entire insurance company organization. There are many more projects on the table than there are people to program requested changes. Time constraints, as well as computer system constraints, play important roles in what can be offered by insurance companies. In addition, insurance products themselves are much more systems-dependent than many other types of business products.

An example of one major project addressed by insurance companies was the "Year 2000" (Y2K) issue. It was a massive undertaking by insurance companies because it affected nearly every facet of their business policy wording, agency contracts, suppliers, and vendors, as well as ultimately requiring that insurance companies made certain that their future policies were issued with the correct dates.

In addition to providing programming for new products, the IT department is charged with maintenance of existing computer systems. This includes updating the software programs, addressing hardware problems that pop up at individual workstations, and solving a multitude of other technological issues as they arise.

Management

It is impossible to talk about an insurance company without mentioning its management. Some companies' top management focus on claims, some on sales, and some on underwriting. As a very general statement, many of the direct writer insurance company top management concentrates more on underwriting, while companies that sell through independent agencies tend to focus more on sales.

Some decisions faced by insurance company management involve federal and state legislation. At times insurance companies attempt to impact future legislation in ways such as having lobbyists express their opinions to lawmakers. However, most of the time insurance companies *react* to legislation that has been passed. Insurance is a heavily regulated industry because it deals with the "public good." As a result, laws pertaining to insurance change frequently.

Unforeseen Circumstances Impacting Insurers

One example of significant change was California's *Proposition 103*, which passed in 1983 and was known as the Insurance Rate Reduction and Reform Act. This law mandated insurance price rollbacks and required insurance carrier prior approval from the California Department of Insurance before any rate adjustments were made. The outcome of this law in the 2020's has been a California insurance availability crisis, with homeowner carriers pulling out of the state. In turn, this has pushed policyholders into surplus lines markets and into California's FAIR Plan.

Another example of an unforeseen factor that has impacted insurance companies includes the *Terrorism Risk Insurance Act* (TRIA), which came about due to the United States terrorist attacks on September 11, 2001. It was first passed in November, 2002, and subsequently reauthorized a handful of times. At the time this book was written, it has been extended until the end of 2027. TRIA requires that the federal government act as a backstop in situations involving severe damage resulting from terrorist attacks.

The last TRIA legislation, passed in early 2015, gradually increased the program trigger from $100 million to $200 million, reduced the government's share of the losses from 85 percent to 80 percent, increased the insurer aggregate retention amount from $27.5 billion to $37.5 billion, and indexed it to the sum of insurer deductibles in years thereafter. If you are interested in learning more about this topic, visit the web for TRIA legislation and access Terrorism Risk Insurance Program–U.S. Department of the Treasury, which can be found at https://home.treasury.gov.

Indeed, legislation has a huge impact on the insurance industry. In addition, the trend has been for regulatory bodies that are responsible for oversight of the insurance sector to become more and more pro-consumer in their approach to dealing with conflicts that arise between insurance companies and consumers.

There are other factors that are beyond an insurance company's control but can have a tremendous effect on its future profitability. New competitors can enter a particular geographic area or introduce a new or enhanced insurance product into the marketplace with very aggressive pricing. Existing carriers may need to match that pricing or risk losing market share. Unexpected catastrophes can strike several different times during any given year. Tornadoes, hailstorms, hurricanes, terrorism, and large losses can deplete a company's surplus.

Large losses are defined differently by each insurance company. For some, it may be a claim that exceeds $10,000 paid out. For another insurance company, it may be defined as losses that exceed $100,000. Rest assured, however, that any loss that reaches the limit of insurance stated on the policy declarations page (generally the first page of your insurance policy–where a summary of limits and coverages are shown) is considered a large loss. When a loss exceeds the limit of a primary insurance policy (the policy that pays first), the insurance company may be required to pay even more if an umbrella policy exists.

So, keeping all the above factors in mind, I have a question. Why do a great number of insurance companies' management obsess over strategic planning as far as five or ten years, or even longer, into the future? I have yet to figure this out.

Of course, it certainly makes sense to develop action plans to address things that are currently happening or things that might happen up to two years or so in the future. Included in this planning process timeline should be things such as the possibility of entering additional states, business product re-focus and the estimated prices (rates) that may be charged for products.

However, my experience has been that insurance company management often spend an inordinate amount of time trying to *guess* what will happen in the general insurance marketplace, what might happen to the overall economy, as well as future government regulation and many kinds of other things, where there is little chance of accurately predicting the outcomes. In insurance, as in life, seldom does anyone correctly guess what the future holds.

How many people correctly called the 2000-2002, 2008 and 2022 bear stock market returns in advance? And did anyone foresee the terrorist attacks of September 11, 2001 that forever changed so many things in the United

States? My point is that you might be lucky enough to have a good guess once or twice, but that is all it is, a guess.

Yet, there exist some management strategists who are so foolish that they believe they can determine long-term impacts that specific future occurrences might have on the insurance industry, and to plan accordingly. Please give me a break! Surely, a better use of management time can be contemplated that will result in directly measurable results to offset their salaries.

One area of management decision-making that I have found particularly disturbing during my career concerns the best way to run insurance company operations. Some companies feel it is best to centralize operations. This means that most of the work (claims, policy issuance and underwriting) will be done out of one centrally located building. A year or so later, these same managers, or perhaps different managers who might currently be running the same company, then decide that it would be best to decentralize their company operations by having multiple operating locations. Back and forth it goes with no ultimate cost savings realized on the insurance company's bottom line.

The coronavirus (Covid-19) pandemic changed how employees worked for some time thereafter. Management allowed workers to do their jobs from home and to use technologies such as Zoom and Microsoft Teams to stay connected with other employees and to interact with customers and potential customers. However, things are changing now with many employers requiring employees to come back into their office location, at least on an infrequent basis. Think about it…can companies with large office buildings keep taking tax deductions for their buildings if no employees work there?

Another area that is constantly changing is how work is done within the confines of the insurance company. An insurance company may choose to have very linear, defined departments. An example of this is a company that has only underwriters in one department, claims adjusters in another department, marketing people in another department, etc. This same company may later decide that it would be good to have teams comprising underwriters, claims persons, and marketing representatives sitting close to each other and interacting frequently. Management might then decide to go back to their original internal structure, or some combination of the two.

Please don't get me wrong. I believe that change can be good–especially at stodgy, conservative insurance companies. However, I have seen too many first-hand examples of significant change predicated upon non-logical, emotionally-based decisions. For instance, a national insurance company opened a large regional office simply because the senior vice-president they had hired to lead the office wanted to be located at a specific city and state within a short drive of his current residence.

Round and round it goes, where it stops nobody in insurance senior management positions seems to know. Inordinate amounts of money are spent changing where business is done and how it is done. In some ways, it appears that the more something costs, the less attention it attracts.

As an example, an insurance company I previously worked for changed our company name only to later find out that it was much too similar to the spelling of another insurance company's name. We were subsequently sued to cease and desist using our new name. Everything that contained our changed name had to be destroyed and we had to rebrand to another name. Think about the time and dollars involved, from reprogramming software to changing contracts and letterhead, and so much more. To this day, I wonder about the ultimate cost of this major faux pas.

I know that mistakes happen. However, how many senior managers, attorneys and others were involved with this initial name change decision? It seems that someone along the way should have raised a red flag before final approval was made.

Another thing that insurance company management is sometimes guilty of is focusing on small, somewhat insignificant matters while losing sight of the big picture. For instance, supervisory level (and lower) company positions at one of my former companies were instructed to take every opportunity to keep expenses down. One way was to avoid spending more than $100 per night at a hotel, while another was to make certain that all travel involving the purchase of airline tickets be scheduled two weeks or more in advance to save on the cost of plane tickets.

Yes, this makes sense. However, senior management at the same company had no such constraints and were free to purchase airline tickets on a whim within 24 hours of their date of travel whenever they wished. This stance negated the savings of several tickets purchased two weeks in advance. To some extent, I understand the saying that rank has its privilege. However, the bottom line is the bottom line. Management should not be above contributing to the financial success of the company.

5.

A Little-Known Factor Affecting Insurance Companies

Most people do not realize how several different areas impact their insurance policies. One such area is reinsurance. How does reinsurance affect the individual or the business that buys insurance? It can affect both the coverage provided in your insurance policy and it impacts the amount of money you pay for your policy. Let's find out how.

Reinsurance

Reinsurers insure the insurance company. The term reinsurer came about from the concept of "re," defined as "once again," as in to reapply a coat of paint. Reinsurers pay for losses that occur under the specific contract that is signed between themselves and the insurance companies that they reinsure. Usually, these agreements provide reimbursement for catastrophic types of losses. Examples of catastrophes that may be reinsured range from widespread losses that occur over a large geographical territory (such as storm damages from hurricanes and tornadoes) to claims involving significant dollar amounts at a specific location (such as damages associated with the September 11, 2001 terrorist actions in New York.)

Reinsurance protects insurance companies from paying out a significant amount of their policyholder surplus (savings) in cases where the insurance company is obligated to pay out very large dollar amounts usually within a very short time. In these situations, reinsurers reimburse companies for amounts paid out. However, reinsurance is, in some ways, nothing more than a loan to the insurance company. When reinsurers make payments to insurance companies, they often recoup their payout in the form of higher prices in future years for the reinsurance they provided to such insurance companies. This approach is similar to what happens to your policy when your primary insurance company increases its prices after you make claims under its policy.

How Reinsurance Works

Insurance companies typically purchase reinsurance based on one of the following methods: *treaty*, *facultative* or *bordereau*, and insurers can use all three methods at the same time. Treaty reinsurance is negotiated across the insurance company's entire book of business according to agreed-upon criteria. For example, the criterion might be losses that fall within a dollar value range between $500,000 and $1,000,000. Treaties include many exclusions. One such exclusion may prohibit the insurance company from binding any business that fills propane tanks on their premises due to the potential of a large loss, such as explosion.

Treaty exclusions can be overcome when the reinsurer grants an "exception" or "accommodation." Sometimes these terms are used interchangeably. Other times, an exception refers to a "minor" allowance of something excluded by the reinsurer, while an accommodation refers to a "major" allowance. Using my propane tank example, the reinsurer will ask several specific, detailed questions and may agree to make an accommodation based upon answers given by the company underwriter pertaining to the specific risk characteristics of the business to be insured. The answers to these questions are obtained directly from the business that fills propane tanks. One of the most important things a business can do if it fills propane tanks is to make certain that their refill tank is located a significant distance (i.e., 100 feet or more) from any other combustible materials–buildings, contents, vehicles, etc. If not, the reinsurer will not make an accommodation.

One ancillary benefit of working with reinsurance companies is the opportunity for insurance company underwriters to gain additional knowledge about the potential risks involved in the types of business policies they underwrite. Reinsurance underwriters are experts in their given fields and freely share their knowledge with the insurance company underwriters that they work with.

Facultative reinsurance is purchased on a case-by-case basis when a specific risk falls outside of values that are contained within the treaty reinsurance agreement. An example is when an underwriter wishes to insure a building valued at $2,500,000. Here, if treaty insurance only allows values of up to $1,500,000 to be insured, facultative reinsurance would be purchased by the underwriter in the amount of $1,000,000.

When facultative reinsurance is purchased, it may require added exclusions and additional premium must be paid to the reinsurer to cover the additional exposure(s) that they have agreed to reinsure. While the purchase of facultative reinsurance was cumbersome in the past, today it is an easier process. Underwriters simply click on an icon on their computer, answer a few questions, and a price for the cost of reinsurance comes back almost immediately. The reinsurance may be immediately bound and the insurance company can add the account to their book of business.

Bordereau reinsurance is purchased when an insurance company wishes to reinsure a specific set of risks. An example of this type of reinsurance is when a book of business is purchased from another insurance carrier and the purchasing company wishes to limit its loss exposures associated with the new book of business by purchasing reinsurance. A book of business refers to the purchase of several insurance policies from another insurance company. Book of business can be defined in a variety of ways, but examples could include one insurance company buying all personal automobile policies or all farm policies from another insurance company.

Make no mistake: reinsurance costs money. With treaty reinsurance, the cost is built into *all* insurance policies written by the insurer. With facultative reinsurance, an additional surcharge is added specifically to the *individual* insurance policy written by the insurance company, based upon individual risk characteristics, and this cost is directly passed along to the business that requires it.

As treaty reinsurance premiums to insurance companies increase, these costs are eventually passed along to consumers in the way of future policy premium increases.

The Impact of Reinsurance on Insurance Market Cycles

A "soft" insurance market cycle can be defined as a period when there are low insurance premiums, higher limits are more freely offered by underwriters, broader coverages are available, and more competitive policy prices exist. Part of the cause of soft insurance markets is due to reinsurance premiums stabilizing or decreasing due to reinsurance company profitability. For the most part, a soft insurance market existed between 2005-2009.

In 2012 and 2013 the soft market began to "firm" (also known as a "hardening" of the insurance market) somewhat, with a notable hardening occurring later, between 2018-2023. As the market firmed, higher premiums were charged to policyholders, along with the implementation of tighter underwriting standards and fewer policies written in standard insurance markets (and more policies written with excess & surplus lines carriers). One factor that affected the hard market was due to poor reinsurance company results, especially those related to property policies. Many weather-related events eroded reinsurance company surplus and caused them to charge higher prices to the insurance companies they did business with. In turn, policyholders saw their insurance costs rise considerably.

If you go back to *Inside the Insurance Industry–Second Edition, © 2011* you will find that I correctly predicted when the current hardening of the insurance market would take place.

I made another accurate prediction in *Inside the Insurance Industry–Third Edition, © 2014,* stating that the hardening market was here to stay for a few years. Further, I speculated that single-digit increases would be borne by many policyholders, but that insurers would not be reluctant to increase prices considerably for those accounts where loss experience had been poor. Additionally, if insureds paid significant insurance premiums (the definition of significant varies from insurer to insurer) and had had good loss history (i.e., no losses for several years), it would be possible to maintain existing pricing levels or to even reduce the cost of insurance in coming years. However, this reduction of insurance pricing would often entail obtaining competitive quotes from insurance companies not currently providing the coverage. Refer also to Chapter 8, "Pricing."

And while I admonished insurance carrier management for future predictions decades out, it does make sense to contemplate what might happen in the immediate future. Therefore, my prediction for 2025–and for a few years thereafter–is that I foresee a gradual softening of the insurance marketplace for most businesses and individuals. However, this is predicated upon a growing USA economy (due to economic and political policies, absence of large-scale war and other negative pervasive events), a robust stock market, and manageable widespread reinsurance losses resulting from natural disasters.

Bottom line: my guess is that the insurance marketplace will soften in 2025, and for a few years thereafter, because carriers have accumulated surplus during the past few years and they are now ready to invest that surplus in further company growth.

6.

External (Third-Party) Resources

Insurance companies and insurance agencies employ several people to help them meet their business directives and to achieve their ultimate goal of profitability. But who works solely in the best interest of the insurance purchaser? Here are two resources that do *not* contract with insurance carriers or agencies.

Public Adjusters

Public adjusters are claims adjusters who work directly with businesses and individuals rather than for insurance companies. Generally, public adjusters are hired in the following circumstances:

- When a significant claim occurs for which the insurance company offers less money than the policyholder feels is due under their policy (policy limit issues).

- When the insurance company tells its policyholder that they will not pay for a loss that the policyholder feels should be covered (coverage issues).

- To facilitate ease of presenting a claim to the insurance company after a large and complicated loss occurs–such as a major fire (coverage expertise and time saving issues).

Public adjusters are consumer advocates who intercede with insurance carriers on behalf of their policyholders. Public adjusters are paid directly by the policyholder and must be specifically licensed in many states.

There are not many public adjusters doing business across the United States. As a result, it is not uncommon for these individuals to travel across the entire country to provide their services.

Insurance Consultants

Insurance consultants provide professional insurance and risk management advice and services directly to clients, often on a fee-only basis. One way to look at this profession is that they provide insurance agent performance appraisals to businesses and individuals.

Think about it. Company employees receive annual appraisals to let them know how they are performing in their job. Good employees are patted on the back, but since no one is perfect, there are also areas of improvement that are mentioned in their performance review. Employees who are not meeting expectations may be put on a formal action plan and may ultimately be let go.

How does a business or individual know whether their insurance agent is doing a good job if a performance appraisal is never completed? Oh sure, plenty of informal and emotionally-based performance reviews are done. But mostly, if an insurance agent remembers your birthday, takes the company CFO golfing once a year, or brings the human resources person responsible for insurance some kind of treat, the insurance agent's informal performance appraisal is that he or she is doing a great job!

Some time ago, I recall seeing an insurance company advertisement that made a lot of sense to me. The tag line was, "Who insures you doesn't matter. Until it does." Luckily, most businesses and individuals never have a claim, let alone a catastrophic claim. And that is a wonderful thing for both insurance company and policyholder alike. But what if a claim does happen?

After the claim occurs is **not** the time to find out that inadequate policy limits were in place, or that you have unwillingly been self-insuring an event that could have easily been transferred to an insurance company.

So, what specifically does an insurance and risk management consultant do? Property and casualty consultants provide exposure analysis and recommendations, assist in marketing selection and im- plementation, and offer other specialized services as the need arises. Below are some specific services provided by a typical insurance and risk management consulting firm.

Exposure Analysis and Recommendations

For an insurance consultant, widely known within the insurance industry as a risk management consultant, the first step often entails conducting a detailed interview with one or more key persons in the business. Key person is generally defined as the owner or a "C-level" position within an organization. This interview process provides the means to identify exposures to loss and permits the consultant to recommend appropriate actions to address the exposures identified during the interview.

Risk management consultants next analyze an organization's insurance and risk management programs and then make recommendations regarding coverage and program administration improvements, as well as suggesting loss control and financing mechanisms. Specific recommendations are provided that go beyond recommending the purchase of insurance products and often focus on areas of pure risk management. Remember, insurance is just one aspect of risk management–it is a risk transfer technique.

Other Specialized Services

Risk management consultants can also provide specialized services such as:

- Claims reviews and audits;
- Safety program implementation and review;
- Litigation support and expert witness testimony;
- Evaluation of third-party administrators;

- Self-insurance analysis and captive insurance company feasibility studies;
- Identification of risk financing options;
- Insurance claims assistance;
- Broker and/or agent selection and review;
- Disaster planning implementation and review.

Another way to look at an insurance consultant is as an "out-sourced risk manager." Nearly all Fortune 500 companies, and many smaller ones, have risk managers on staff to perform the duties mentioned above. Smaller companies may be unable to afford a full-time risk manager but could welcome outsourced assistance from a risk manager who provides services on an as-needed basis.

7.

Insurance Litigation

Until the time I was about 30 years old I believed that many of the people who sued others were money-grubbers and were simply out to make a buck. After all, why couldn't most people simply get along and solve their differences without aid from our legal system?

But as I aged, I came to understand why individuals and businesses wanted their day in court. The United States was founded on principles that include equitable treatment and due process, and sometimes, it becomes necessary to address issues via lawsuits.

For instance, if a manufacturer makes a product that harms its customers, knows that it harms their customers, and takes no action to recall its product and to improve defects due to potential costs of doing so, little can be done to change the manufacturer's behavior other than for the government to force a change via existing laws, or for an individual to sue the manufacturer.

A judgment against the manufacturer often causes it to make changes for a couple of reasons. First, a court finding against the manufacturer compels it to acknowledge the possibility of wrongdoing and is generally accompanied by a change in behavior–such as modifying a dangerous product. Second, if it does not change its behavior, the manufacturer becomes susceptible to additional adverse judgements for the same reason, including the possibility of punitive damages, where allowed.

Lawsuits are common in the realm of insurance. Insureds sue their agents and insurance companies. Insurance companies sue their insureds and their own agents. Businesses sue other businesses due to required contractual insurance provisions that were not met, and many other types of legal actions exist that are related to insurance.

During the past several years I have become more and more involved in providing advice to attorneys, typically after a lawsuit has been filed. I have been involved on both plaintiff and defense sides of the table and can attest that both sides usually have a supportive argument.

> **But know this**: in most situations, insurance lawsuits come about due to a **communication failure** of some type.

Several of my cases pertaining to insurance defense work involve insurance agent negligence. I have often been hired by insurance companies that provide Insurance Agent Errors and Omissions insurance coverage to the insurance agency and to the specific insurance *agent* accused of some type of negligent action or inaction.

While insurance agent responsibilities vary from state to state, several states hold that it is the responsibility of insurance *buyers* to tell their insurance agents what coverages and what limits of insurance are desired. In essence, the insurance agent is charged with "taking the order" of their customer. Of course, this relationship is situation-dependent and can be altered depending on things such as the length of time the insurance customer and insurance agent relationship has been in effect, whether the insurance agent gives proactive advice and holds himself or herself out as an expert, whether fees in addition to commissions are charged, and other factors.

However, where a typical insurance agent and customer relationship exists, the insurance agent's primary responsibility is simply to procure (obtain) the insurance coverage that their customer tells them to order and to tell their customer in a timely manner if they are unable to obtain the policy that was ordered. Let me repeat this statement to avoid any misunderstanding: the insurance agent's foremost task is to obtain the insurance that their customer has ordered. After obtaining the policy, insurance agents should provide at least a cursory review of the insurance policies that have been issued so that they can determine whether what was delivered fulfills what was ordered.

Cases that involve supporting the plaintiffs usually occur after there has been a series of discussions between the insurance policyholder and the insurance company claims adjuster. Sometimes, the insurance company determines at the onset of a claim that coverage under the insurance policy (contract) may not apply. In these situations, a reservation of rights letter is sent to the insured policyholder before any other action is taken by the insurance company. In these situations, insurance company defense may or may not be provided to the insured. However, since the duty to defend an insured is one of the most important duties that an insurance company owes its insured, a stance not to provide defense is taken very seriously by the carrier.

I have seen some situations where an insurance company's actions are absolutely appropriate, in my opinion. On the other hand, I have also seen insurance carriers make poor decisions (i.e., wrong coverage determinations) and then dig in their heels when there is little, if any, support for their position. In these situations, insurance companies have a built-in advantage in the legal system. They can deny coverage, and so long as they have a "reasonable" explanation for their position, they can hold onto the money that they would have paid on the claim until such time that a court determines that the claim *must* be paid.

Bad Faith

The term "bad faith" resulted from courts holding that there is an "implied covenant of good faith and fair dealing" in all contracts of insurance. This is because insurance contracts have special characteristics. They are *unilateral* (drafted by only one party–the insurance company) and *aleatory* (the contract is based upon the insurance company's promise to pay for a future unknown event).

The burden of proof is on the plaintiff to prove that bad faith should apply, and generally a negligence standard pertains to bad faith cases. In other words, if a plaintiff can show that **another insurer would not have** reasonably denied or delayed payment of the claim under the same facts as the defendant insurer did, then the defendant insurer may be guilty of acting in bad faith.

First-Party and Third-Party Bad Faith Claims

States vary in how they address bad faith claims. Some recognize both first-party insurance bad faith claims and third-party insurance bad faith claims, some do not. The term "first-party" refers to the insured who is protected by the insurance policy. The term "third-party" refers to third-party claimants and many times involve excess verdicts.

First-Party Insurance Bad Faith claims may involve an unreasonable delay or unreasonable denial of payment of a claim. The words "reasonable" and "unreasonable" are generally not specifically defined and may be determined in a court of law (where a jury is oftentimes involved) based upon specific facts of the case at hand. If an insurance company's actions are deemed unreasonable or inappropriate based on the facts of the case, a bad faith claim may be brought forth by the insurance policyholder's (plaintiff) attorney.

If an insurance company has committed bad faith, then the policyholder can be entitled to damages, such as breach of contract damages, attorneys' fees, and punitive damages (if allowed). Punitive damages are meant to punish and deter an insurance company from future similar bad acts. Some states allow punitive damages and some states do not.

Depending on the state where the alleged wrongdoing took place, and the specific situation involved, an allegation of bad faith in the Complaint may change the case from contract to tort. This is because the insurance company's actions are no longer based upon the insurance contract itself, but become based upon the breach of the implied covenant of good faith and fair dealing. Once a bad faith tort action is initiated, the damages sought may no longer be limited to the damages that would have been owed by the insurance company under its insurance policy.

Most states impose a duty on the insurance company to exercise ordinary care (due diligence) in *all* aspects of handling claims. Some situations require special attention by claims departments to avoid allegations of bad faith. A couple of these include excess verdict cases (those above the policy limits) and high dollar claims that may or may not be covered under the insurance policy.

Claims departments must use care when a claim may exceed the limits of the policy. While it appears that carriers could simply pay the policy limit and exit the case, courts have determined that since these claims may put the insured's personal assets at risk, additional care is necessary by carriers. For instance, adjusters must use sufficient care to evaluate such claims and must keep the insured apprised of negotiations and other pertinent claim information throughout their handling of the claim file. Obtaining feedback from insureds prior to any settlement is also important.

When a claim adjuster determines that a claim may not be covered under the insurance policy, it is important that they send a *reservation of rights letter* to their insured stating that their initial determination is that no coverage applies to the loss at hand, but that they are willing to entertain additional information that could change their mind. This becomes especially important when a denied claim involves a substantial amount of money.

Note: It is important to understand that the area of bad faith can differ dramatically from state to state and that these types of lawsuits are always dependent upon the specific facts of the case at hand. Bad faith claims are generally difficult to prove, and insurance companies are typically absolved of wrongdoing if they have a reasonable basis for their position and/or actions. It is also important to understand that all of my comments related to the area of bad faith are intended to be a *general* introduction to this topic. Should you desire additional information in this area, please consult with an attorney who is well-versed in this specialized area of the law.

Sample Litigation Engagements

I mentioned at the start of this chapter that I have been involved in many insurance-related court cases. So that you might gain a better understanding of the types of things that are litigated in the insurance arena, below are examples of some cases that I have been involved in during the past several years.

Defense Cases

- **Failure of Insurance Agent to Recommend Specific Trucker's Insurance Coverage**

- The plaintiff alleged that the defendant insurance agent held themselves to a higher standard and failed to recommend coverages that would have applied to a loss that occurred.

- **Failure of Insurance Agent to Provide Product Recall Insurance**

  - The plaintiff alleged that the defendant insurance agent promoted himself as an expert in commercial insurance but failed to offer product recall coverage to the defendant's business. A loss occurred involving product recall and the plaintiff had to pay for resulting costs out of pocket.

- **Architects' and Engineers' Professional Liability Insurance Wrongful Placement Based Upon Application Information Provided by the Business Customer**

  - The plaintiff alleged that their insurance agent obtained incorrect professional liability insurance based upon improper application information he relied upon when obtaining the insurance policy.

- **Insurance Agent Responsibilities in the Areas of Application Completion and Issued Policy Review**

  - The plaintiff alleged their insurance agent missed the completion of information on the application and did not review the issued policies, resulting in gaps in insurance coverage that were paid by the defendant.

- **Application of Intra-Family Exclusion on a Specific Recreational Vehicle Coverage Endorsement**

  - The plaintiff argued that their insurance agent did not explain an exclusion on their policy that denied coverage for the exact situation that occurred after their policy was written. Damages had to be paid directly by the plaintiffs.

- **Insurance Agent Duties Related to Home Replacement Cost Determination**
  - The plaintiff alleged that their insurance agent had the responsibility to determine the replacement cost value of their home since he was in the best position to do so. A total loss occurred and the insured plaintiffs were responsible for amounts over their policy limit.

- **Failure of Insurance Agent and Insurance Company to Properly Write Builder's Risk Loss of Income Coverage**
  - The plaintiff business argued that both their insurance agent and their insurance company mistakenly changed the business income policy limits without input from them. A major loss occurred and the business income limit was insufficient.

- **Failure of Insurance Consultant to Recommend Uninsured Coverage for Personal Vehicle Driven in Florida**
  - The plaintiff argued that the insurance agent held himself out as an expert and therefore should have offered a specific coverage available in the state of Florida. Since the coverage was not added, the plaintiff was responsible for an out-of-pocket payment.

- **Lack of Property Insurable Interest and the Resulting Impact Upon Property Insurance Coverage**
  - Insurance carrier denied a claim due to the plaintiff's lack of insurable interest. Plaintiff sued their agent alleging he had a duty to inform them about the ramifications of insurable interest on property policies.

- **Failure of an Insurance Agent to Submit a Customer's Directors and Officers (D&O) Claim to the Insurer**
  - The defendant insurance agent failed to submit a potential D&O policy claim on behalf of their insured's business. This

lack of notice became the basis for a denial by the insurance carrier and defense coverage, and limits of insurance that the plaintiff believed were in effect were denied by the carrier.

- **Insurance Agent's Negligence in Failing to Write an Insurance Policy That Was Allegedly Requested**

    - The plaintiff alleged that his insurance agent did not write an insurance policy that he had requested on a rented house. A fire occurred and there was no insurance policy to pay for damages incurred.

Plaintiff Cases

- **Bad Faith Claim Handling Involving Insurance Company Duty to Defend**

    - The defendant insurance carrier allegedly mishandled their insured's claim along with failing to pay their attorney's fees.

- **Denial of Water Damage Claim Within a Commercial Apartment Building and Resulting Mold Damage**

    - The plaintiff alleged that their insurance company's incorrect denial of their water damage claim resulted in additional damages to their home, including mold.

- **Claim Denial Due to Property Vacancy and Improper Insurance Company Interpretation of the Vacancy Condition**

    - Insured business argued that their insurance carrier improperly denied coverage for water damage to their building due to an incorrect interpretation of their insurance policy wording.

- **Insurance Agent Failure to Offer Employment Practices Liability Insurance**

- Insured contractor alleged that his insurance agent did not discuss the addition of Employment Practices Liability coverage to his insurance policy. An employee alleged wrongdoing by the contractor and no insurance coverage applied.

- **Improper Cancellation of Farm Insurance Policy**
  - Policyholder alleged that the insurance carrier did not follow proper procedures dictated by state law when cancelling his farm insurance policy. A loss subsequently occurred and the carrier denied coverage.

- **Inadequate Insurance Limits Due to Insurance Company and Insurance Agent Negligence**
  - The plaintiff argued that both his insurance agent and insurance company changed his building replacement cost limits of insurance without his knowledge or approval and his business suffered damages when a fire loss occurred that exceeded his policy limits.

- **Insurance Company's Improper Denial of Their Insured's Fire Damage Claim**
  - The plaintiff sued their insurance carrier for denying damaged that occurred from a fire. Bad faith was also alleged by the plaintiff due to their carrier's claim denial.

- **Bad Faith Due to an Insurance Company's Improper Handing of a Business Income Claim**
  - The plaintiff alleged monetary damages due to their insurance carrier's mistakes in applying incorrect policy interpretations during the handling of their business income claim.

- **Insurance Company's Denial of Business Income Damages Due to Covid-19 Business Shutdown**

- The plaintiff argued that due to the wording of their insurance carrier's business income coverage, their policy should have provided payment for the shutdown of their business due to Covid-19. Instead, their carrier denied coverage due to a lack of direct physical damage.

8.

Pricing

One of the basic premises behind insurance is the *Law of Large Numbers*. This refers to the idea that as more exposure units join a statistical group, losses become more predictable. In other words, insurance companies attempt to spread the losses of a few among the many who pay insurance premiums.

In the past, I had a conversation with my own insurance agent concerning a dramatic 35 percent increase in my homeowner policy price. He said that the insurer had experienced several catastrophic losses during the year and that they needed to increase prices to stay solvent. This is an example of the Law of Large Numbers at work.

Insurance companies attempt to write policies to insure individuals and businesses with risk exposures that will not have losses, hoping to earn an underwriting profit. An underwriting profit occurs when premiums paid into the insurance company total more than the losses paid out, plus the expenses incurred, by the insurance company. It does *not* include other sources of income, such as investment income.

Here's the rub. The typical insurance consumer does not know whether he or she is adequately covered or whether they are paying a fair price in the marketplace for what they have purchased. They rely almost exclusively on what their insurance agent or insurance company tells them. This can be a big mistake!

Insurance companies tell agencies that represent them not to "leave money on the table," and management at these insurance agencies pass along the same message to their sales force. This means insurance agents should try to sell insurance policies at the highest possible price while still closing the deal. In personal lines (such as automobile and homeowners) there are often pricing "tiers" that customers may qualify for. These are controlled by underwriting guidelines, for the most part, but exceptions can be made to give customers a better deal than they would normally qualify for.

Equate this to paying the sticker price for an automobile rather than obtaining a discount for the car you purchase. Many consumers have no idea that they may be able to qualify for a better price with the same company. Remember, it is in the insurance company's best interest to charge the highest possible price for their products since this helps improve their bottom line.

In commercial lines (i.e., businessowners, commercial property and general liability coverage) there is even more rate (price) flexibility. Technically, underwriters are charged with looking at the characteristics of a particular business and applying "credits" or "debits" to that specific business. However, policy pricing can also depend upon non-risk characteristics.

One such non-risk characteristic is the market cycle. In soft markets, most policies have some type of credit, and pure underwriting credibility can be lost. In this cycle, credits tend to be applied haphazardly with little regard to the actual risk characteristics of a business, so that a certain low price can be reached to write the account. Bottom-line pricing is king in soft markets.

In hard markets, the pendulum swings the other way and consumers are often charged more than their individual risk characteristics might merit. As mentioned in the last chapter, this may be due to the increased price of reinsurance, or perhaps due to the insurance company having poor results in a previous year–for example, their combined ratio (defined as the ratio of income to expenses) was over 100 percent.

And sometimes, pricing a new business account amounts to nothing more than an underwriter asking their agent (or the client directly) how much the client is currently paying with their incumbent insurance company–and then releasing a quote at a slightly lower price. This lower price is typically low enough to entice the prospective customer to move their insurance, but generally is not as low as the company could go.

Special Pricing Tools Used for Business Policies

There are special tools available to business underwriters when they price accounts. Experience rating allows certain types of commercial business (also known as "lines" of business) to be further discounted, depending on an individual account's specific risk characteristics, such as past loss history.

A-rates are "judgment" rates applied to certain general liability codes which allow the underwriter to price this line of business however they wish (using their best judgment). For instance, if I want to insure 1,000 acres of real estate development property (land), the judgment rate could be anywhere from .01 per acre to $100 or more per acre.

Loss costs are additional rating factors that are used by underwriters during the premium rating process. Loss costs are often applied to commercial liability or automobile business policies and reflect the insurance company's profitability within these lines of business. For instance, loss costs can be applied separately to commercial automobile liability, automobile comprehensive, automobile collision, and other factors that make up the total premium for commercial automobile insurance. Generally, insurance companies can apply additional credits by using loss costs. However, if debits result from a carrier's loss costs the resulting price may be adverse, thereby making the line of business uncompetitive.

General liability rates are usually based on sales (receipts), units, acres, or such similar measurement. General liability rates are filed with state Departments of Insurance based on "class codes," which differ according to the type of business being insured. As an example, a frozen food distributor has a class code of 13049, while a restaurant with no sales of alcoholic beverages–without a dance floor–has a code of 16814. Different types of businesses have different corresponding base rates.

Property rates are usually developed from Insurance Services Office (ISO) inspections. ISO, or other organizations, physically inspects properties and provides insurance rates for insurance company use. These rates are based upon factors such as the building construction (i.e., frame, masonry, non-combustible), and fire protection (i.e., less than five road miles from the responding fire department or more than five road miles from the responding fire department). The developed rates are then accessed by insurance company underwriters who make an educated guess as to the probability that this particular property will be a good risk for the insurance company to insure.

The higher the probability of loss (i.e., a wooden building located fifteen miles from a responding fire department), the more premium on a "rate per $100 of value" basis the business or home owner will pay, if the reinsurer even allows the insurance company to write this type of high-risk property. Alternately, the better the risk from a fire protection standpoint, the lower the rate per $100 that will be charged, such as when a business building has a masonry exterior, has fire hydrants within 50 feet of its premises, and is located two blocks away from the responding fire department.

Commercial Automobiles are generally priced based on the type of vehicle (i.e., "heavy"–over 20,000 pounds), the radius of operation (i.e., "intermediate"–51 to 200 miles), whether there is a fleet (5 or more units), and the business usage (i.e., "service" vs. "commercial" use). In addition, underwriters look at motor vehicle records of all persons who will be driving vehicles for the business.

Introducing IRPMs

Along with pricing tools such as experience rating and loss costs to apply credits on an account, IRPM (internal rate premium modification) factors can be applied to reduce the "manual" rate developed. Underwriters use their judgment when applying IRPM. Some insurance companies have internal guidelines with breakdowns related to when, and how much, IRPM can be applied.

Insurance companies generally must file their IRPM factors with the state departments of insurance. For instance, an insurer may file an IRPM with a 40 percent debit (surcharge) and a 40 percent credit (savings) that is applicable to their property business rates. Figure 1 is an example of how an underwriter can apply credits and debits:

Credit

Number of Years of Management Experience = 5:	5% credit
3 Year Loss History = Less than 50% (10% actual):	20% credit
Positive Company Financial Data (i.e., D&B report):	15% credit
Total Credit Applied:	40% credit

Debit

Age of Building Less than 20 years (45 years actual):	-15% debit
Fire Hydrant Less than 1,000 Feet (3,000 ft actual):	-10% debit
Years in Business More than Three (One yr actual):	-10% debit
Total Debit Applied:	-35% debit

Figure 1. Example of applied IRPMs

Underwriters are generally given authority to apply a limited range of credits or debits. But underwriting supervisors or managers have higher authority levels. Underwriters can build a business case for additional credits or debits and then approach their supervisor or manager for approval. My experience has been that some people at higher levels freely agree to sign off on an underwriter's request, while others rarely do. Often, it is a matter of trust. When a supervisor or manager signs off on additional credits, or otherwise gives an exception to write an account that is outside of the underwriter's authority, they are held accountable by their boss if that account has losses.

Concerning worker's compensation (work comp) policies, many of these policies offer dividends as an incentive for a business owner to write their work comp with a particular insurance carrier. While dividends are not guaranteed, they have a strong history of being paid on a regular basis. In addition to offering various dividend plans, some states allow companies to discount their rates through use of IRPM credits.

Why Your Business May Not Be Desirable to an Insurer

While covering the area of pricing, it is important for you to understand that there are factors that can impact your personal or business insurance pricing that are beyond your control. One such factor is the decision by either insurance companies or insurance agencies, or both, to consider certain policyholder characteristics that you cannot change. For instance, an insurance company may decide that although the company once freely wrote insurance on restaurants, it no longer is interested in insuring these types of businesses.

This might be due to a senior manager, who is new to the insurance company, having had a bad experience with restaurant losses at a previous employer. He or she then decides that it is no longer in the best interest of their current insurance company employer to insure restaurants.

As a result, an edict is sent to all underwriting staff to begin to "run off " (not renew) restaurants that the company insures. This can be done in different ways, but usually involves applying significant price increases at renewal.

Nothing about the restaurant has changed; its only sin is that it is no longer considered desirable from the insurance company's current viewpoint. Eventually, the insurance company's restaurant policies book of business may be sold to another insurance company that does not harbor similar negative feelings about restaurants.

A similar circumstance can take place at an insurance agency where, through no fault of your own, you begin to be treated differently. Why might this happen? One reason might be that, with the hope of improving their insurance agency profitability, they hire a third-party strategist (consultant). One of this consultant's suggestions may be that the agency should begin segmenting their business by premium volume (or commissions earned).

This aligns with a school of thought espousing that insurance agencies need to spend more time with accounts that pay higher premiums and that the smaller accounts are a distraction. Therefore, the agency picks a number, for instance accounts that generate above $25,000 annual premium for commercial lines of business. Accounts that generate less are handled strictly by customer service representatives and are not considered for any agency accommodations. The idea is for the agency to give these customers the very least amount of time possible, and if the customer happens to leave, that is perfectly okay with the insurance agency.

As a business strategy, these insurance companies' and insurance agencies' actions cannot be faulted. They are entitled to run their businesses the way that they desire. My issue with these types of insurance company and agency actions is that customers are seldom told about these new strategies. Therefore, if you do not pay close attention to how you are treated by your insurance company and/or insurance agent, significant changes may be taking place that can cost you money.

As an insurance consumer, it is in your best interest to stay alert and to notice when significant changes are made to your insurance coverages and/or pricing, and to ask questions. Things can change over time and purchasers of insurance become complacent and wrongly have the opinion that their insurance company and insurance agent will always have their best interests at heart.

If you find that your business is no longer welcome at your insurance company or agency, shop around. You are likely to find another insurer and agent with a different business stance that will happily provide insurance to you.

Your Mindset Matters When Saving Money

One last thing before leaving the topic of pricing. Let's return to the example of the automobile industry and how cars are sold. Manufacturers need to obtain a bottom-line price on models they sell to cover their expenses and to remain a going concern. Similarly, dealerships need a certain amount of profit (typically a percentage of gross revenues) to keep the doors open. However, their sale price varies from vehicle to vehicle, even for the same model. There are people who pay sticker price for their cars and there are people who are ferocious negotiators. In the end, dealers net out *all* sales for their bottom line. Some customers pay more, some pay less, and the dealership makes enough money to cover their expenses and to obtain a reasonable margin of profit.

It is much the same for insurance companies and insurance agencies. Some people accept whatever pricing their insurance company and insurance agent deliver, while others negotiate every single policy's insurance premium. Overall, both the insurance company and insurance agency make enough money to stay in business even though prices paid may differ from customer to customer.

It is your choice to decide which type of insurance purchaser you wish to be when it comes to the cost of the insurance policies that you purchase.

Refer to the next chapter, How to Get the Best Insurance Deal, for additional information related to the cost of insurance policies.

9.

How to Get the Best Insurance Deal

I have always been fascinated by how people spend their money. Some spend $100 or more during one night at the bar while throwing $1 into their weekly church collection basket. Some feel life experiences are worth thousands of dollars while others feel travel is a waste of their hard-earned money. Some live paycheck to paycheck and spend nearly all the money they earn, while others save 30 percent or more of their pay. I am not making any value judgements here–I simply want to point out that people have very different views on spending money. And on saving money.

Full disclosure: personally, I have always been a saver. For instance, I feel it is worth spending some of my free time researching automobile information prior to purchasing an auto so I can save a few thousand dollars or so. And I spend time considering ways to save money on the purchase of insurance policies for myself and for my clients.

If you are not interested in saving money on insurance, feel free to skip this chapter. But if you would like to save money on insurance and to put that savings into the bank, or have it available for another use, read on.

Insurance is confusing even to those who have made it their avocation. Incorporating the definition of risk management found in chapter one, what can an insurance buyer do to protect themselves from financial harm at the lowest feasible cost? In other words: get the best product at the most reasonable price? Of course, using a good consultant is invaluable to help you wade through insurance jargon but there are also common-sense things that can be done by everyone–regardless of whether you have any insurance expertise.

Be Cautious When Purchasing Insurance Without an Agent

In my opinion, one of the scariest things today is insurance sales over the internet or through direct mail because the person selling such policies may have limited insurance knowledge. I have personally contacted companies that offer insurance products over the internet and through direct mail, and I have found that the representative selling insurance products lacks technical knowledge. Often very simple questions are confusing to them. For instance, I asked the representative to explain "automobile medical payments" coverage to me over the telephone. He failed miserably. Not only did he not explain the coverage properly, he provided incorrect information. This type of situation is like the blind leading the blind when neither the person selling insurance or the person buying insurance have a good understanding of coverages.

The main advantages of internet and direct sales methods are price and convenience. However, there are exclusive agents and independent agents who can sell at or below prices being offered over the internet or through the mail. The key is that you must find them. Certainly, the convenience of the internet and direct mail is an attractive factor. However, this can be countered with use of email, a fax machine or by visiting web pages of insurance agents or consultants. Go ahead and get a quote from the internet companies, but do not make your insurance policy purchase decision until you have completed your due diligence, which includes comparing their policy coverage and pricing to what other insurance companies offer you.

9 | How to Get the Best Insurance Deal

How do you go about finding a good insurance company or agent? It is easy to find many insurance agents and agencies listed on search browsers and you can sort them by a variety of criteria, including: location, insurance companies represented, reputation and more. Referrals are also a method of getting names; however, as mentioned earlier, you should not place too much weight on the fact that someone was referred to you. You should still interview the person thoroughly before allowing them to become your insurance representative.

This is a good place to mention a caveat. The intent of this book is not to provide a summary of a few significant steps that will allow every reader to purchase the very best insurance coverage for the least amount of money. That objective is impossible to achieve because there are too many variables at play. Situations vary from individual to individual and from business to business. Therefore, what might be best for one person's situation is not best for someone else's.

Also, understand that insurance coverages can vary considerably from insurance company to insurance company. Something as seemingly simple as "property coverage" encompasses a great number of differences between carriers. I have spent my entire professional career learning about coverage differences and it is simply not possible to share my knowledge about insurance policy coverages in a few sentences, a chapter, or even a book.

But there are most certainly things that you *can* do to obtain better insurance policy pricing and improved coverages for yourself–and this book will absolutely help you do that. Understand, though, that this will require some work on your part. One way to look at this is you may be able to save $500 on your home and auto insurance by spending five hours working on your personal insurance program. And, likely save even more on your business insurance policies. That equates to $100 per hour for your time spent on personal insurance alone. Not a bad monetary return for time invested. The other benefit of going through this process is that you will learn new things about insurance. And more knowledge is a very good thing.

Two Very Important Areas When Quoting Insurance

Keep these two things in mind as you obtain insurance quotes:

- **The limit is the limit**. While some "enhancements" may apply to certain coverages, it is best to focus on the limit of insurance that appears on your policy declarations pages. The limit of insurance is generally the most that will be paid for losses that occur. It is a good idea to quote higher limits to determine how much it costs to buy increased limits so you can decide if the additional cost is worth the higher amount. You may be surprised how little higher limits cost.

- **Buy an umbrella policy**. There has been a trend of higher dollar case verdicts. In fact, over a ten-year period the number of cases with verdicts over $100 million increased by 400%. If your personal liability, auto liability or other policy to which an umbrella applies has insufficient limits, the amount over your insurance limit may need to be paid by you.

Before you quote an umbrella policy it is important to know what you are buying. Those in the insurance industry sometimes label policies as an "umbrella" when, in fact, they may be "excess" policies. Excess policies are intended to provide only higher limits over underlying policies while umbrella policies may provide additional coverages *and* higher limits over underlying policies.

Specific Steps to Decrease What is Paid for Insurance

Here are specific steps that you can take to reduce the amount of money that you pay for insurance:

1. **Prepare a summary of insurance coverages and limits of insurance that you desire for each type of insurance policy you wish to purchase.**

   For instance, if you want to obtain competitive homeowner policy quotes, develop a spreadsheet template that includes the following coverages and limits of insurance:

   - **Coverage A (Dwelling)**
   - **Coverage B (Other structures)**
   - **Coverage C (Personal property)**
   - **Coverage D (Loss of use)**
   - **Coverage E (Section II liability)**
   - **Coverage F (Medical payments)**

   Other Coverages Desired (i.e., flood insurance, sewer backup, inland marine, etc.)

   A good starting place is to look at your current insurance policy's declarations pages, which provides a summary of your existing coverages and limits. Then contemplate whether the stated limits of insurance meet your needs and whether you have concerns about any of the policy coverages, policy limitations, exclusions, or endorsements. If so, jot these down, research them and discuss these with the insurance agent who writes–or wants to write–your homeowner insurance policy.

> One area of special concern with homeowners' insurance is the limit of insurance written on your home (Coverage A-Dwelling). If your insurance agent is an order taker, you alone are responsible for determining your home's limit of insurance. However, insurance agents and insurance companies often have access to software programs that can help determine a reasonable current home valuation, so ask them to provide this to you.

A caveat: garbage in, garbage out applies here. If incorrect information is provided by you, such as an incorrect square footage and/or other wrong criteria, the limit of insurance that was estimated will be wrong. Also, know that just because your insurance agent provides a replacement cost "estimate" for your house, it is still your responsibility to consider whether you ultimately agree with it. If you have concerns, you can always contact a homebuilder or hire an appraiser to confirm your home's insurance replacement cost valuation.

Other personal insurance policies can be approached the same way as the homeowner policy. Other personal policies include: automobile, umbrella, personal articles floaters (also known as personal inland marine), watercraft, and recreational vehicles.

2. **Contact several different insurance agents who represent different insurance companies. Include direct writers and independent insurance agencies and get quotes from at least two different insurance companies.**

Depending where you live, there may be many insurance agents and many insurance companies that can offer insurance for your situation. If so, be methodical in your approach and first choose insurance companies that will best fit your unique situation. For instance, if you own a home valued at one million dollars or more, Chubb, AIG or Cincinnati may be good companies to consider.

Next, choose "top-tier" insurance agencies that represent such companies. Sometimes, you can determine such agencies when you conduct your internet search because agencies like to advertise this honor. Other times, you will need to speak to an agent at the insurance agency and directly ask them whether they are recognized as a top-tier agency or if they have earned other types of carrier recognition.

If you live in a geographical area that is considered "coastal" or that has some other type of negative insurance situation, you will be hard-pressed to find competitive insurance carriers for your home or business–especially for homeowners or property insurance. But you may still be able to identify insurance companies that can provide other types of competitive insurance policies, such as personal automobile, or if you own a business, a competitive general liability insurance policy.

This is a good time to discuss insurance for large businesses. While large businesses can be defined differently, I will define them as those that generate over $1,000,000 of combined insurance account premium annually. When businesses generate such insurance revenues, large insurance brokers are often involved in providing insurance policies.

Large insurance brokers include companies such as Marsh McLennan, Aon, Willis Towers Watson, Arthur J. Gallagher, Brown & Brown, and HUB. These types of large brokers do not like to compete against each other on price; rather, they like to sell insurance based on what their firm can offer to customers. Services can include pricing models, analytics, loss control, claims assistance, and more. But make no mistake, these brokers often compete on price if this is necessary to write the insurance.

One of my clients was spending several million dollars on their property & casualty insurance program and wanted to reduce their premiums by a substantial amount. My consulting firm helped them save a million dollars in premium by going through a bid process pitting large brokers against one another. So, even though brokers do not like to compete on price and coverages, large businesses that purchase insurance via a competitive bidding process are almost always glad they did so.

3. **After receiving insurance proposals, it is time to begin evaluating which insurance agents and insurance companies seem likely to provide you with the best policy.**

By now you will start to feel which insurance agency and company may best suit your situation. Things such as your initial interaction with the insurance agency, their customer service and turnaround time and the pricing you received all play a part in your ultimate choice. Additionally, you may want to formally interview the agent you will be working with in the future.

Some questions to ask a prospective insurance agent include:

- How many years have you been a licensed agent or consultant?

- What do you consider to be your "specialty" (strongest area) and why?

- What are your weakest areas? How do you deal with those areas?

- What can you offer me that other agents cannot?

- Who writes your personal insurance coverage? Many of the best agents have others write their own coverages so they have a second set of eyes to review their policies, as well as to have someone else to sue if improper coverages are written.

- How important is continuing education to you? What is the last class you took?

- What is your opinion concerning the future of the insurance industry? Give a brief description of what you feel it will look like two years from now.

- If I do business with you, who will be handling my account? You, one of your customer service representatives or someone else in your office?

- What can I expect from you in the future? How often will you review my account? What is your renewal process?

- What types of services can you provide besides selling insurance policies?

- Provide the names and phone numbers of five of your most satisfied clients.

- What is the best method to communicate with you? Email, telephone, fax (fax is making a comeback), cell phone or other?

- Name the five largest insurance companies your agency represents (by premium volume), and what are their A.M. Best's ratings?

- Taking my situation into account, would one of these five insurance companies do a good job on my account? If not, do you represent another carrier that would be a good fit? Tell me about them.

- How well does the company you are proposing to write my insurance handle claims? What is their claims reputation? Are they "slow payers" or "tough payers?"

Separately, I suggest you visit your state's commissioner of insurance website to research the agency and the individual insurance agent who you are interested in working with. You can access whether they have had prior insurance complaints, whether their insurance license is active, if they have met their continuing education requirements, and more.

4. **Next, enter all information received into your spreadsheet. At this point you can begin excluding insurance companies, narrowing your choice down to two or three insurance companies and the agencies that represent them.**

    You may wish to refer to the Sample Quote Spreadsheet that I have included in this book's Appendix.

5. **Dig deeper into the coverages provided.**

    - Ask the insurance agent you may be choosing to explain coverages that were quoted.

- Ask what differences exist between their insurance quote and what other insurance companies are offering.

- Ask the insurance agent to identify significant coverage limitations and exclusions that reduce or eliminate coverages.

- Ask about coverages that apply to any specific exposure that you are concerned about. For instance: swimming pools, trampolines, dog breeds, woodburning stoves, solar panels, antiques, firearms, musical instruments, or anything else that you are concerned about insuring properly.

6. **Access your state's Department of Insurance Information for Additional Helpful Information**

Each state has their own website that provides a lot of consumer-related information, and most do a good job of sharing a variety of important materials.

For instance, the State of Wisconsin's Office of the Commissioner of Insurance (OCI) website, which can be found at https://oci.wi.gov, contains information such as:

- A "lookup" feature to investigate individual insurance agents, insurance agencies, insurance companies and public adjusters.

- How to file an insurance complaint against insurance companies, agencies, or agents.

- Ask the OCI staff a question about insurance.

- Learn about various areas of insurance, including consumer alerts, cybersecurity, and the ability to access consumer publications.

7. **Register for an A.M. Best account**

It does little good to buy an insurance policy from an insurance company that is having financial difficulties. And while "Guaranty Funds" exist to help make policyholders of defunct insurance carriers whole, I recommend avoiding this process, if possible.

One way to ascertain the financial strength of an insurance company is to visit https://web.ambest.com and register for an account with AM Best. AM Best is the world's largest insurance industry-focused credit rating agency. You can not only review carrier information such as the size and financial strength of insurance companies, but also find parent insurer and subsidiary company information.

8. **Choose an insurance agent and insurance company.**

   After following the above steps, it is time to act. Make choices based upon objective, empirical data and try to keep subjective opinions based upon how an agent looks or acts to a minimum.

9. **After you receive your insurance policies, review them to make certain that what you ordered has been delivered.**

   You would not believe how many errors I have found over the years when reviewing insurance policies delivered to my clients from insurance companies. The law in most states is that you have a duty to read your insurance policies. Of course, this does not mean that you must have a strong understanding of all the insurance language in your policies. But it does mean that you need to have a level of understanding of your policy that a reasonable person in your same circumstances and with similar educational and career background would have.

Introducing the RISC Analyzer

If you would like help identifying *personal* or *business* exposures that you may wish to insure, or to identify risks that you may want to retain, consider buying a license to use the **RISC Analyzer**. For more information and to obtain access to this program visit www.riscanalyzer.com.

The **RISC Analyzer** program helps you identify and evaluate your exposures to financial loss through a series of probing questions. Identified exposures can then be retained or addressed with your insurance agent, attorney, or financial advisor.

A unique aspect of the **RISC Analyzer** is that it explains *why* the questions asked in the program are important, which helps you avoid the negative financial consequences of failing to transfer or knowingly retain identified risks.

For example, one of the questions asked is, "Have you had any real (or personal) property formally appraised during the past three years?

Here is the reasoning provided: A key concern of P&C insurers is obtaining adequate premium for the exposures they insure. A major component in this regard is the amount of insurance carried on property that is insured. While most losses are partial losses, it is important to consider the fact that a total loss can occur and to purchase a limit of insurance high enough to protect against this possibility.

If you are interested in using the **RISC Analyzer**, email us at marketing@riscanalyzer.com. A discount is available for verified purchasers of this book.

Perhaps An Insurance Consultant Can Help

Now that you know how to improve your insurance coverages and insurance policy pricing, the question remains: Will you follow through on taking these steps?

Based upon my experience more people will answer "no" than will answer "yes." Why? Most people do not want to invest the time necessary to obtain positive outcomes. Others just don't "like" insurance and would rather ignore coverages and the price they are paying for their current insurance policies.

But since you have purchased this book, you are more likely than the general public to give attention to your insurance policies. However, even you may feel uncomfortable with the technical aspects of insurance coverage or may not desire to spend a great deal of personal time on improving your current insurance situation.

If this describes you, there is another alternative: hire a fee-only insurance consultant.

Based upon direct feedback from clients, I can attest that insurance consultants play the role of "the great equalizer" in the insurance purchasing process. Fee-only consultants do not represent any insurance companies and work entirely on behalf of their clients. There is no dual fiduciary responsibility conflict since fee-only consultants do not sign contracts with any insurance companies.

Insurance consultants are free to recommend any insurance company that will do the best job for your specific needs. Some of the benefits realized by personal insurance and business insurance consumers when using a consultant include:

- Specialized knowledge
- Ability to obtain broader coverages
- Ability to obtain lower prices
- Time savings for client
- Impartial second opinion of current insurance program, including agent and insurance company effectiveness reviews

How Much Does an Insurance Agent Earn?

Before leaving the topic of pricing, I would like to share some other information that is not common knowledge. First, how much do you think an insurance agent or insurance broker earns annually?

You may be surprised by the answer. While each insurance agency is free to compensate their agents or brokers any way they wish, generally there is some type of commission split involved with seasoned agents and brokers. The agency/brokerage keeps part of the commissions earned for both new business and renewal business while the individual agent/broker receives the rest.

For instance, when a commercial property insurance policy or a homeowner's policy is sold the commission earned is generally around 20 percent. Of this 20 percent, the agency may keep 5 percent the first year and then 10 percent in subsequent years. The higher commission initially paid to the agent/broker compensates them for the additional efforts needed to write new business policies. The lower commissions in subsequent years helps pay for "back-end" agency support.

Good insurance salespeople earn a good living. Earnings of more than $100,000 annually are commonplace, with $250,000 per year somewhat routine. Further, some of the agents and brokers who specialize in businesses that pay high premiums are making over $1,000,000 per year.

This is no different than other occupations where the worker specializes in high-end services. For instance, I ate at a higher-end restaurant and had a lengthy conversation with the restaurant manager afterwards. He freely offered that some of his waiters were earning more than $100,000 per year in tips alone–and this restaurant was operating in a medium-size Wisconsin city.

My experience has been that insurance salespersons (also known as "agents" and "brokers") are some of the best salespersons around–especially those working at large agencies and brokerages. They establish relationships with their clients and are the type of people that others want to do business with.

Some have limited insurance knowledge because their primary job is usually to sell insurance and then help to maintain relationships with the insurance buyer afterwards. The technicalities of insurance are handled by others within the agency/brokerage, e.g., by Account Managers, Account Executives, or someone else with a similar title.

One other item of note relates to commercial accounts that are paying more than $150,000 annually for their property and casualty insurance, excluding worker's compensation. At this premium size, the account can generate more than $15,000 in commissions (assuming an average 10 percent commission on all policies written) for an insurance agency. In this situation, a business can request that the insurance agency "contribute commission" to offset the quoted $150,000 premium. Here, the insurance agency tells the insurance company to reduce their commission by X percentage and to apply this commission reduction to offset the quoted premium.

Why would an insurance agency do this? Well, some won't. They feel they are entitled to earn full commissions. But others do not have a problem doing so for several reasons. First, a consultant may be involved and he or she performs many of the information-gathering duties that an agent or broker would otherwise do–thus saving them considerable time. Another reason is that the lower price may persuade a client to choose their agency, and a lower premium earned is better than no premium.

I know of one Minnesota agency that built their book of business by writing *every* account on a "no-commission" basis. Their agreement with their clients was that they would forego commissions the first year but then earn full commissions in subsequent years. This approach worked well for this specific agency and they grew quickly.

The last item to touch upon in this chapter involves writing accounts on a "net of commission" basis, where no commission is taken by the agency. Instead, there is a separate agreement between the agency/brokerage and their business client stating how much money the agency/brokerage will charge for services rendered during the policy year. Ultimately, this dollar amount may be more or less than the agency/brokerage would have earned on a commission basis. Note that this approach is generally used on accounts that pay higher premiums.

10.

More on Risk Management

As discussed in chapter one, insurance is just one aspect of risk management—it is a risk transfer technique. Risk management is a broad discipline and a full discussion of this topic is beyond the scope of this book. However, it is important to understand some basic risk management concepts to better understand how insurance fits within risk management parameters.

It is also important to understand where risk management and individual risk managers fit within a typical business organization. But do not be confused about the title "Risk Manager" or the function of risk management within a business. Too many times I have been referred to a company's risk manager only to find that this person's true job is human resources, purchasing, accounting or some other position where they are responsible for meeting with the company's insurance agent, managing the insurance renewal process, and turning in the company's claims when losses occur. Many people in these roles lack technical insurance and risk management knowledge and instead function in a quasi-clerical role.

Refer to the chart on the next page for an illustration of the structure of a Risk Management Department within a medium-to-large-sized company.

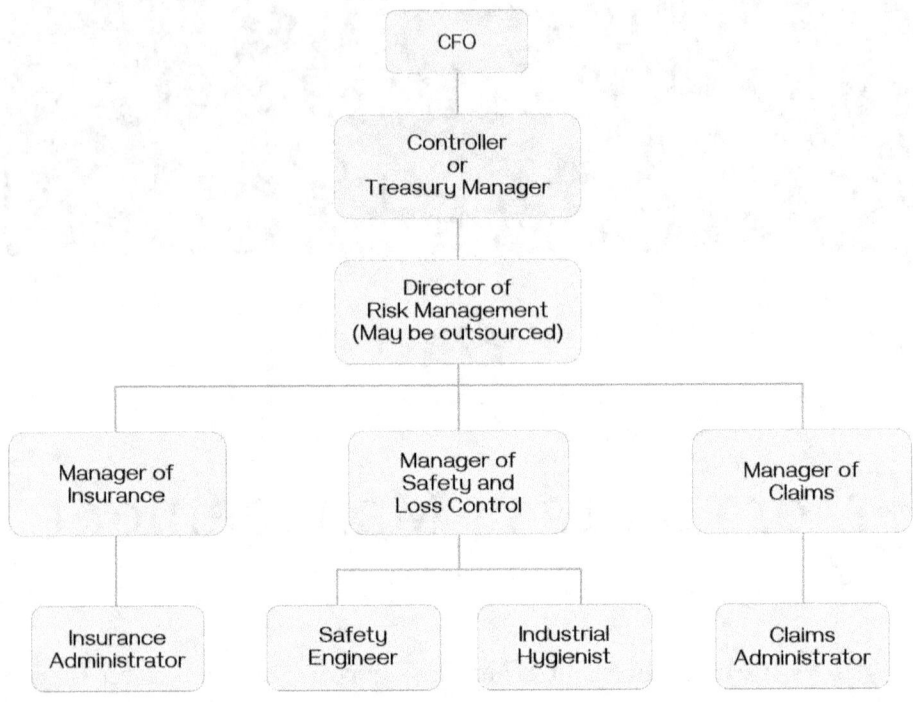

Figure 2: Sample Risk Managment Department Organization Chart

Understand that the Risk Manager can perform the duties of the positions located below his or her role, or can supervise individuals who fill these positions.

I have also included two additional items to provide a more complete understanding of risk management. The first is a list of a risk manager's essential responsibilities. It explains the typical duties and responsibilities of a risk manager within a general business setting.

Second, a risk management case study has been included in the Appendix section of this book. This case study provides insight into how a risk manager analyzes a specific business situation and provides sample answers to questions related to the case study.

Since outsourced risk managers do not work for insurance companies or brokers, they can keep in mind the best interest of only the company that hired them. And outsourced risk managers have a fiduciary duty to keep the best interest of their business client in mind when making decisions concerning the best risk management course of action that will ultimately be taken for their client's specific business operations.

Outsourced risk managers are typically the primary point person when corresponding with the client's insurance broker and insurance carrier. This includes bid processes and issues that arise between insurance carrier underwriters, claims adjusters and more.

Risk manager decisions should be objective, but sometimes clients use emotional or subjective reasoning when making decisions. For instance, I was hired as a risk management consultant on a project for a large, complex contracting enterprise. Part of the scope of my project was to discern whether the business should have one master policy with all subsidiaries named in the master policy, or whether more than one insurance policy should be written providing coverage for one or more of the subsidiary companies.

During my project, I discovered that there was a wood furniture manufacturing business that had low revenues, high losses, and seemingly no redeeming qualities. Therefore, I recommended that not only should the furniture business be written on a separate policy, I also strongly suggested that the parent corporation consider selling the furniture business.

Ultimately, the decision-maker at the parent company said that he understood the reasoning for my recommendation. But this furniture business happened to be founded by the parent company's majority stockholder's great-great grandfather, and it held significant sentimental value to him. As a result, they decided to make no change with regards to their furniture business.

While personally disagreeing with this course of action, I fully respected my client's decision.

Risk Manager Essential Responsibilities

A risk manager brings a unique set of valuable skills to a company. The following list is a sample of essential services a risk manager can provide:

- Researches, compiles, and maintains insurance placement and renewal application underwriting information.

- Negotiates and recommends the procurement, renewal, budgeting, and record-keeping of all corporate insurance.

- Analyzes coverage options, prepares, and presents recommendations for placement.

- Guides the establishment and implementation of loss control-related operating and training procedures between business units and brokers/insurers.

- Conducts site visits to identify risk exposures, maintains a working knowledge of applicable codes and standards and recommends appropriate loss control solutions.

- Manages the day-to-day risk management and insurance functions, ensuring that corporate policies are followed and amended as business needs change.

- Identifies changes in corporate risk exposure. Coordinates issuance of insurance certificates.

- Assists the internal audit manager (or CEO, CFO, etc.), in the development and maintenance of risk management policies, procedures and programs necessary to mitigate identified corporate risk exposures.

- Assists in the analysis and identification of risk exposures associated with contracts or agreements between the corporation and any contractor/vendor, including leases.

- Provides risk transfer recommendations to mitigate company exposures.

- Assists the Legal Department with claims management, administration, and settlement.

- Assists the Human Resource Department as a loss control liaison related to safety and health, medical and Worker's Compensation claim areas.

10 | More on Risk Management

- Maintains and analyzes loss experience data and recommends appropriate policy changes.

- Provides corporate insurance perspectives to governmental regulatory agencies, code officials, and insurance companies as required.

- Represents the corporation in appropriate regulatory or public safety forums.

- Performs miscellaneous ad hoc analysis as required.

- Develops and communicates risk management policies.

- Conducts risk identification surveys to identify risk exposures.

- Arranges alternative risk financing solutions (in addition to insurance), where appropriate.

- Implements/monitors loss control program.

- Determines cost of risk and prepares applicable allocations to cost centers.

- Participates in due diligence analysis related to mergers and acquisitions.

- Designs, implements, and monitors claims handling and loss control procedures.

- Develops and maintains a risk management policy and procedures manual.

- Develops and maintains a risk management information system to identify, measure and manage risk within the organization.

- Conducts alternative funding feasibility studies to identify costs and benefits of implementing transfer mechanisms beyond traditional insurance programs. Includes analysis of alternatives such as captives or self-insurance, or joining association-owned insurance companies.

- Reviews, analyzes, and monitors overall risk management department operations, including program results and effectiveness.

- Organizes and administrates third-party self-insured provider contracts and performance.

- Coordinates risk management policies with organizational mission and goals.

11.

Evolving Areas in the Insurance Industry

My grandfather was a wise man and I often think back to some of his pearls of wisdom. For example, "when it comes to work, one boy is a man but two boys are half a man." He was referring to when two boys are together, they talk as much as they work. Another was, "money is hard to make but easy to spend." With an ancillary reminder that once money is gone, it's gone. And he often lamented on the many dramatic changes that occurred during his lifetime of 79 years, which began in 1901.

While he indeed saw many changes when he was alive, it was nothing like the transformations that I have seen so far in my lifespan. Which, I am sure, will be nothing like the dramatic changes that will occur in generations to come.

It is important to acknowledge that the past decade or so has seen a great number of changes that impact the insurance industry. Each of the areas identified in this chapter could be the subject of a separate book–or at least a lengthy chapter on each. But my intent here is to simply introduce you to some of the areas that are becoming more prevalent today that were not as commonplace at insurance companies when I wrote *Inside the Insurance Industry – Third Edition*.

One such significant change involves more frequent use of *Parametric Insurance*. This is a financing tool that may be utilized by insureds to hedge against higher deductibles on their insurance policies. It is based on agreed-upon coverage triggers, and is typically considered for perils such as Named Windstorm or Hail. This product can be used to cover previously uninsured exposures.

Parametric insurance (also known as index-based insurance) is not traditional insurance. Instead, it involves an insurance contract that pays a specific dollar amount based on the magnitude of an *event* versus the magnitude of the *losses* that would be paid under traditional insurance policies.

For example, rather than an insurance company providing coverage for specific damage up to a limit of $1,000,000 for an insured's building resulting from an event such as a Named Windstorm, the contractual agreement may state that a flat $1,000,0000 amount (the parameter) will be paid if the Named Windstorm occurs and meets agreed upon maximum sustained wind speeds in a specific location. The event must be verified by an independent third-party, such as the World Meteorological Organization (WMO) or another agreed-upon independent third-party.

One of the benefits of parametric insurance is the simplicity of claims payment for both the insurer and the insured. If the event occurs, the limit is paid. There is no need to "adjust" a claim or to apply standard insurance policy provisions. For example, wording such as "payment on an actual cash value basis until repairs have actually been made" does not apply.

However, significant problems with parametric insurance exist for both the insured and the insurer. One issue for insureds is that their expectation of payout may differ significantly from the actual payout, or lack of payout. This is referred to as "basis risk." For the insurance carriers, major areas of concern include determining how best to insure the parameter and how to charge for the parametric contract. Thus, parametric insurance requires a high degree of underwriting expertise with a strong understanding of the exposures that the insured contract is subject to, in addition to the parameters that are involved.

11 | Evolving Areas in the Insurance Industry

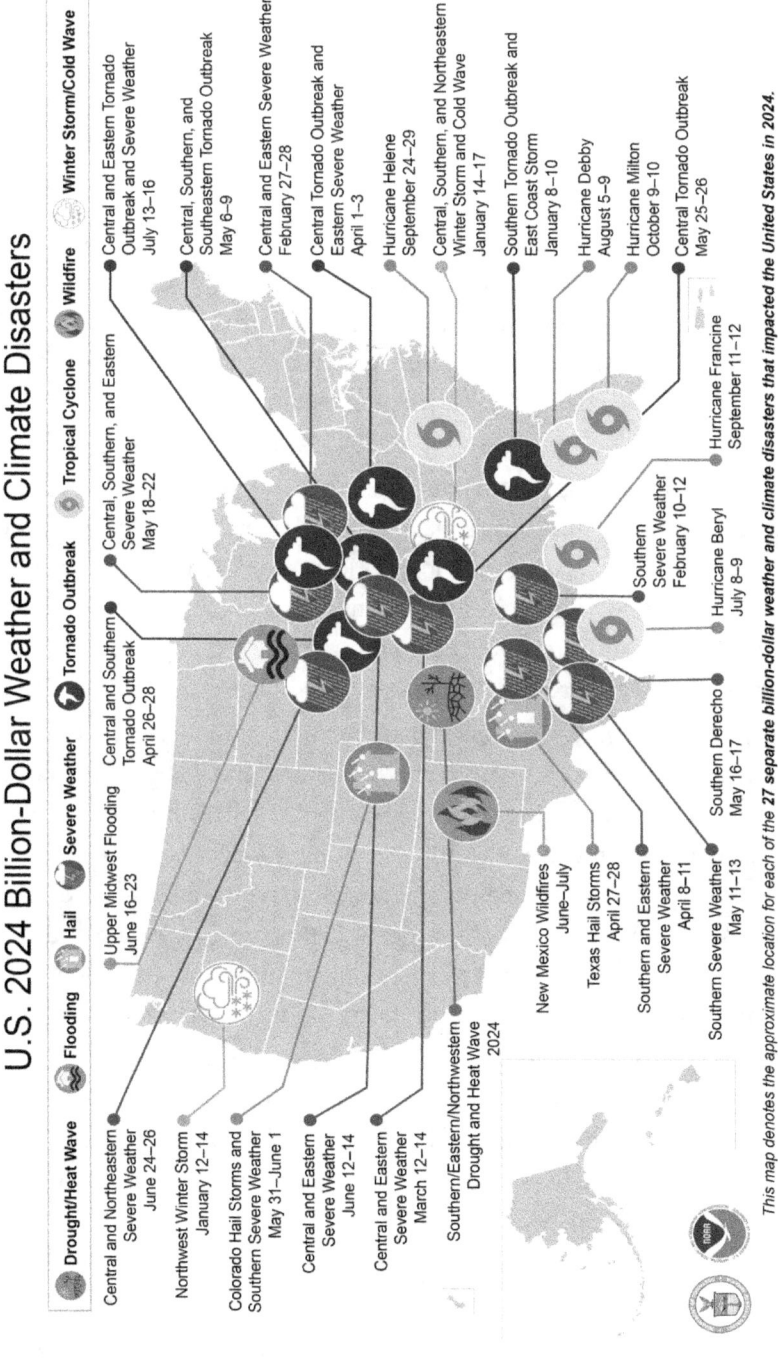

Map and damage information courtesy of NOAA National Centers for Environmental Information (NCEI) U.S. Billion-Dollar Weather and Climate Disasters (2025). https://www.ncei.noaa.gov/access/billions/, DOI: 10.25921/stkw-7w73

Another significant area of insurance change involves *climate-related risks*. Insurance companies are addressing such risks by embracing green technology, such as LEED (Leadership in Energy and Design) buildings, insuring homes with solar panels, and giving attention to other energy-saving construction methods.

Whether or not you believe that human activities related to things such as automobile emissions, byproducts from the production of gas and oil, industrial smog, and more have changed our climate, there has been considerable discussion concerning the impact of these types of actions on the weather. Regardless of the cause of weather changes, it is difficult to ignore that climate changes have, indeed, occurred.

The older you are, the more likely that you can recall how different the weather patterns were as a child compared to today. Years ago, we typically had four distinct seasons and severe weather was far more unusual than normal. These days, the seasons are much less typical, with higher temperatures often experienced during winter months in the Midwest, and with extreme heat occurring during summer months due to a projected depletion of the ozone layer. People generally refer to these combined changes as "climate change."

More so, natural disasters have become more frequent and more destructive. In the last several years, exposures and values associated with losses have increased. Things like megaprojects, with values of $1 billion or more, have become more commonplace. Such projects can involve things like renewable energy (i.e., solar farms), new skyscrapers and additional coastal properties, all involving heavy property exposures. These are but some of the growing list of property exposures that insurers are writing and risking payment for losses should weather-related damages occur.

Thus, insurance carriers have a keen interest in the severe weather that has taken place in the past several years. To try to gain a better understanding of the frequency and severity of future natural catastrophes, insurers have begun using tools such as climate change catastrophic risk modeling and analytics.

In addition, insurers are supporting insureds who are interested in participating in energy-saving initiatives intended to reduce pollution, such as homeowners who install solar panels on the roofs of their homes and businesses that use green, environmentally friendly building materials that meet the United States Green Building Council's LEED green building standards.

Yet another insurance-related product that is becoming wider known involves a type of financial instrument. You may have heard the term *catastrophic bond* (CAT bond) and wondered what this has to do with the insurance industry. A CAT bond is a financing instrument used by both property & casualty primary insurance carriers and reinsurance companies to transfer risk to investors. Its purpose is to generate funds for insurers and reinsurers to offset their payment for catastrophe-related losses. CAT bonds are tied to pre-specified events and payment is made to insurance or reinsurance carriers only if a catastrophe occurs that is protected by the bond.

While selling CAT bonds is beneficial to insurers and reinsurers, why would anyone want to buy a CAT bond? For one thing, CAT bonds often pay higher interest rates than other types of bonds. Also, the length of the bond is generally short (i.e., one to five years) and this investment can be a hedge against other types of financial investments. But those who purchase CAT bonds must be aware that it is possible to lose their entire investment if costs of the covered natural disasters exceed the total dollar amount raised from the bond issuance.

Another term that is becoming more commonplace these days is *risk modeling*. Just as "risk management" is defined differently by different people, risk modeling is also being defined in various ways by people both inside and outside of the insurance industry.

For those working in insurance, the term risk modeling is often intended to mean "predictive modeling," where future pricing of insurance policies take past information into account. And modeling is also known as a method utilized to price out the cost of capital for carriers impacted by catastrophic risks and their treaty reinsurance that is affected as part of the limits being provided.

Years ago, two of the most significant aspects of underwriting a specific account was the account's frequency of past losses and its severity of past losses. These criteria are still part of the underwriting equation today, but additional characteristics are now considered as well.

Software has enabled underwriters to now weigh factors such as location of risk, predictions of expected losses on peril-by-peril basis, inclusion of property classification definitions, specific risk exposure to catastrophes, and more, in their risk-specific pricing—in addition to a risk's loss frequency and severity information. This helps carriers better determine appropriate limits and pricing in an attempt to avoid overexposing the carrier should a major catastrophe occur.

But be advised that some people in the insurance industry refer to the term risk modeling but really mean nothing more than reviewing an account's prior loss frequency and severity.

One more term that you are hearing bandied about everywhere, and the insurance industry is no exception, is *artificial intelligence* (AI). AI refers to technology that enables computer systems to accomplish tasks that previously required human intervention. And just as AI is being used for a multitude of business functions in many different industries, AI is also being used in the insurance industry.

But it is important to realize that AI is nothing new to insurance companies. Long before the phrase "artificial intelligence" was popular, insurance companies have been finding ways to improve efficiencies in areas such as underwriting and claims. In the underwriting process, if certain risk characteristics are met—such as a building being less than 10 years old, located in fire protection class one through five, with no prior losses—the policy might fall within the boundaries of a "guaranteed issue" policy that can be issued without underwriter involvement.

On the claims side, if a claim meets criteria such as property damage only, no bodily injury involved, and less than $2,500 in total claim amount, the claim might be paid without any significant involvement from a claims adjuster.

More and more underwriting and claims information is being fed into computers attempting to widen existing limitations that allow processing without human intervention. And it is not just underwriting and claims departments that are impacted by AI. Clerical work provided by the policy services department is becoming more streamlined in areas such as insurance policy quality control review.

But while it appears there is no stopping the use of AI in the insurance industry, some concerns are starting to be expressed. For instance, the State of Colorado has passed "The Colorado AI Act," which goes into effect in early 2026 that insists those who develop or use certain AI systems must use care to protect consumers from any known or reasonably foreseeable risks of algorithmic discrimination or bias.

12.

The Future of Insurance

In this chapter I will share some thoughts about how the future of insurance may look.

In the prior chapter several things were mentioned as evolving areas that are currently impacting the insurance industry. Of the topics mentioned, artificial intelligence will provide the greatest degree of change. Eventually, there will be no department left untouched by AI's impact and insurance companies will employ fewer and fewer people doing the same jobs they are doing today.

Insurance Jobs That May Be Less Impacted by AI

What if you are reading this book and are already working in the insurance industry or would like to work in the insurance industry in coming years? Which jobs might be safe bets for future employment?

In my opinion, the more complex the work that you do in your job, the safer your position. For instance, insurance companies will have a difficult time allowing computers alone to make underwriting decisions about insuring a business generating $1,000,000 or more in premium, and they will be concerned about allowing computers to settle claims involving bodily injuries with $1,000,000 or higher policy limit demands. The higher dollar amounts that are involved generally indicate complexity, with several different aspects that must be considered. And these types of situations are seldom "yes or no" or "black or white" situations. Usually, negotiations are required to complete the task–and computers are not known for their ability to negotiate…at least, not yet.

Also, if you have "signature authority" at an insurance company (meaning you can hold the company legally liable for contracts), you are probably safe. These positions generally help set the future direction of the insurance company and these are the people who decide how AI is used at their companies.

In my last book I predicted that the trend toward more government regulation will continue. Since insurance represents a large part of a typical household's budget, remains confusing to those outside of the insurance industry, and is concerned with the public good, it cannot and will not be ignored by lawmakers.

My prediction was that more government regulation would continue, which has been the case. However, I also predicted that McCarran-Ferguson (the law established in 1945 which gave individual states the authority to regulate their own state's insurance industry) would be struck down in whole or in part, and that the federal government would become more active in the regulation and standardization of insurance across the United States–much like the implementation of the Affordable Care Act (Obamacare) for healthcare.

While McCarran-Ferguson has not yet been struck down, I still believe it may happen if the direction of the United States continues to move more and more towards big government. If it does happen, individual states will remain active, but they will eventually take a back seat to Washington.

Also, the federal government will continue to offer some type of legislation to safeguard insurance company assets in the event of a terrorism-related catastrophe. I made this prediction while working on my first edition of *Inside the Insurance Industry* in 2005 and this prediction has rung true. The Terrorism Risk Insurance Program Reauthorization Act (TRIPRA) was passed in 2007 and extended the initial Terrorism Risk Insurance Act (TRIA) through December 31, 2014. It was last extended in 2019 and is scheduled to expire in 2027. I trust that it will be extended again.

Easy-to-read policies first appeared many years ago. These should have been called "easier-to-read" policies because they remain difficult for consumers to read and understand. This is true even though many states require certain Flesch reading ease test standards be achieved by insurance company policies, as well as insisting on a minimum size point type (i.e., ten point).

Insurance companies will continue to find ways to make their contracts easier to comprehend by people unfamiliar with insurance. More and more policies will be issued on a businessowners type of policy (BOP) and fewer and fewer commercial package policies (CPP) will exist. This has been occurring gradually over the years as insurance companies expand their underwriting guidelines to accept higher values and a broader array of industries in their BOP programs. Look for this expansion to continue in years to come.

Another reason that I foresee a proliferation of BOP policies is because these will be easier to use with AI. Interestingly, quite some time ago I came across a 3-page BOP policy issued by Berkshire Hathaway. It had headings such as "The coverage we provide your business under this policy," "If something goes wrong," "What we do not cover," and a couple more provisions. I am not aware that this type of policy has gathered much traction, but perhaps it will be making a comeback sometime soon.

Alternative distribution channels will continue to make considerable headway in future years. People will feel more and more comfortable buying over the internet and over the telephone for both personal insurance and small business insurance.

Insurance will continue to be viewed as a "commodity" by consumers and price will remain the number one key consideration in the average person's decision to purchase an insurance policy, regardless of how hard insurance companies and agencies try to sell broadening of coverages and ways that their companies differ from the competition.

In fact, I predict that coverages and relationship with insurance companies and/or salespersons will become an even further distant second and third place.

The trend towards "bigger and bigger" will continue. The lines between banking and insurance and mutual funds will become further and further eroded. Currently, there are insurance companies that own banks, banks that own insurance agencies, insurance companies that own accounting firms, and so on. So, it will become more difficult to tell the difference between the large financial services companies because all of them will offer a broad array of financial-based services.

Consumers will be able to do one-stop shopping. You will have the ability to have your checking account, savings account, money market mutual fund, car loan, mortgage, brokerage account, stock mutual funds, auto/home/business insurance all at the same institution. It will be the battle of the big companies to get *all* the consumer's money from financial services-related businesses.

Eventually, this trend towards huge financial conglomerates will backfire. There will be some consumer backlash and resulting fallout from these big business customers. People will be unable to get in touch with a warm body who can answer their questions at these mega companies. Customer service in general will deteriorate, and people will start viewing large insurance companies much like the government—as a behemoth with lots and lots of red tape, and from whom it will be nearly impossible to get a live, knowledgeable person to address their problems.

In time, people will balk at their inability to access decision-makers at these large financial institutions and there will be a trend towards smaller companies again, or at least large companies that are very decentralized and that operate out of smaller regional offices.

Computers and other forms of personal technology, such as smart phones, will certainly play a more important part in the insurance industry in the future. Cell phone apps will become more and more popular and consumers will make even greater use of technology to receive and to make changes to their insurance policies. Texts and emails will become the preferred method of communication between purchasers of insurance, their insurance agents, and even their insurance carriers.

While the use of artificial intelligence will be applied to smaller and less complex underwriting and claims situations initially, the push by insurance companies will be to have computer software do more and more of the decision-making because this will save them money. At some point in the future, computers may make nearly all claims and underwriting decisions.

Insurance companies will eventually require consumers to complete their own applications for insurance and to submit these directly to the insurance company without insurance agent intervention or assistance.

The compensation model for insurance agents will continue to be at the forefront of discussions between insurance companies and their sales representatives. Insurance companies will want more work done by agents for less commissions paid. Insurance agents will want to do less work for more commissions. There will ultimately be fewer and fewer small insurance agencies. More and more mid-size and large insurance agencies will merge to create huge insurance agency organizations that will rival the size of some regional insurance companies.

Different agency models will be tried. Currently, one of the largest brokerages in the world has segmented their business into large accounts and middle-market accounts. This is similar in nature to the business operations of smaller agencies where they allot resources differently for smaller premium-generating accounts versus large premium-generating accounts.

As insurance companies work more closely with their customers, the role of insurance agents will evolve. Insurance agencies may move from the role of "distributor" of insurance policies to that of "creator" of insurance policies–thereby actually competing against insurance companies for the insurance consumers' dollars. This may start with the introduction of specialized insurance products for unique or segmented businesses and will eventually expand into other, more standardized areas of insurance.

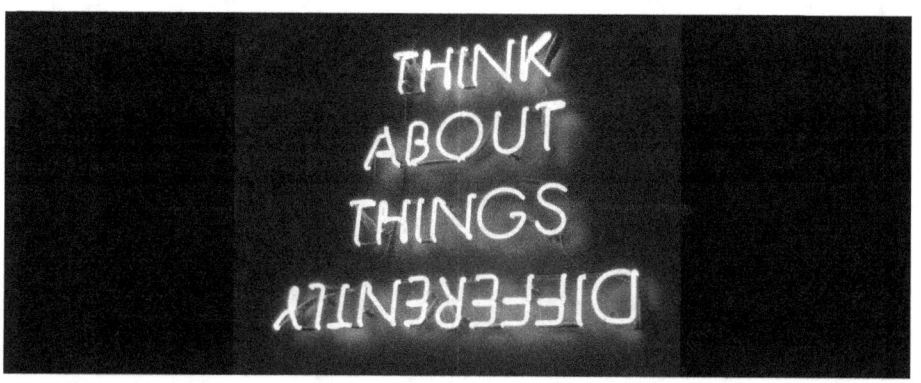

Epilogue

An important reason for writing this book was to provide readers with valuable information about the inner workings of the insurance industry. If I have educated you by shedding light upon areas of an industry that confused you, I have met this goal. As you have read, there are many facets involved with the insurance industry, and the better you understand how the industry works, the better you can protect yourself from potential problem areas that can occur throughout the purchase, maintenance, and claims-making areas of insurance.

I realize that I have shared a great deal of information throughout the pages of this book, and you may be wondering what things I consider to be the most important of all. With the qualification that this is not an exhaustive list, and that the focus here is on purchasing insurance, below are some **key points** that are valuable to keep in mind.

1. Ask the insurance agent specific questions.
2. Document in writing information that you have been told, and retain this information.
3. Know that you have a responsibility to tell your agent coverages you desire and limits of insurance you want.

4. Understand that your agent and insurance company must often be encouraged to save you money on the policies that you purchase. One good way to do so is to obtain competitive quotes.

5. Never lie on insurance applications. And if you do not understand a question, ask for clarification. If you answer a question incorrectly, your insurance coverages might be denied and/or your policy may be cancelled.

6. Have the agent quote a true umbrella policy, when possible.

7. Review your insurance policies after they have been issued and received by you. Mistakes happen frequently and you may be deemed to have accepted the incorrect coverages or limits if you say nothing within a certain period after policy issuance.

8. Do not be afraid to reach out to insurance experts for assistance if you or your company have complicated situations and are paying substantial premiums.

But another reason that I wrote this book is to serve as a wake-up call to the insurance industry. There are many good people doing many good things at insurance companies, insurance agencies, and elsewhere in the insurance industry. And insurance most certainly serves a vital purpose. Without insurance, there would be a tremendous strain throughout society, as people would not be able to financially recover from catastrophes that inevitably will occur.

In addition, people would spend such an inordinate amount of time worrying about what might happen in areas such as property or liability losses that they would not be able to turn their attention to other worthwhile endeavors, including managing their busy lives and running their own businesses.

Yet, I am disappointed—and even ashamed at times—that my industry has not adequately addressed several important consumer issues. Issues such as truly easy-to-read policies, making insurance pricing more understandable to the public at large, and sharing information about payments associated with their distribution systems—including contingency commissions.

And they can also do a much better job of providing more transparent details to policyholders in areas such as why their customers' policies might be cancelled, and explaining specific factors that directly impact the cost of insurance policies that are purchased by its policyholders.

It is my earnest hope that insurance companies will feel an obligation to address these types of consumer-related areas where they are currently weak and will begin to make improvements in these areas.

Let me be clear: I am proud to work in the insurance industry. Insurance allows individuals and businesses the ability to survive financial disasters by either receiving direct claims payments or by receiving initial payments followed by subsequent payments as allowed by provisions in the specific insurance policy that was purchased. In fact, without insurance the financial stability achieved throughout a lifetime of savings might disappear as the result of a single catastrophic event. But insurance carrier improvements can and should be made.

When the above-mentioned positive changes take place within the insurance industry, I and all who work within the insurance industry will be able to hold our heads higher and will be even more proud to shout out to others that we are associated with one of the most important and influential industries ever created.

Appendix

Two samples appear in this Appendix. The first is an example of how an insurance consultant looks at a customer's business from an insurance and risk management perspective. If you are not a business owner you may find the information presented somewhat confusing. As a result, feel free to skip this section.

But if you are a business owner, I encourage you to put yourself in the insurance consultant's role and to spend some time going through the case study.

The second sample is an Insurance Proposal Comparison Worksheet. It is intended as an example to help make sense of how your own unique insurance proposal comparison might look.

How a Consultant Looks at a Business Risk

The consultant's crucial starting point is the identification of exposures. Next, it is important to determine how to address the exposures identified. Remember that insurance is only one possible way to tackle identified risks of loss.

As a result of completing the case study you should better understand ways to improve your business operations, as well as ways to make your company look more desirable to insurance companies.

Sample 1: <u>Western Wooden Products, Inc. Case Study</u>

Western Wooden Products, Inc.

Your customer is the president and CEO of Western Wooden Products, Inc. (WWP), a large privately held furniture manufacturing and repair business. They have been in business for 30 years. Sales revenues have been steadily increasing over the past five years and they now generate $150 million in annual sales and the company enjoys a healthy balance sheet.

WWP employs 250 people in the state of Wisconsin; several salespersons have offices in their homes and some of them are in states other than Wisconsin. One or more salespersons is in each of the following states: Iowa, Michigan, Ohio, Minnesota, and California.

WWP has a triple-net lease in effect. The owner of WWP formed a separate company, Products Building Leases, LLC (PBL), which owns one 100,000-square-foot manufacturing building that is insured on a replacement cost basis for $25,000,000. It was originally built in 1990, but was completely updated (electrical, heating, plumbing, and roof) in 2023. It is fully sprinklered and is situated in Protection Class (PC) 4. There is also a storage building that contains lumber used in WWP's manufacturing process that is located five miles away from the manufacturing building.

The title to this property is also in the name of PBL. The storage building was built in 1970 and has not been updated. It is in PC 10. It has 50,000 square feet and is valued on an Actual Cash Value (ACV) basis at $1,000,000.

Business personal property is located solely at the manufacturing facility–except for lumber and several pieces of machinery and equipment, such as forklifts, which are kept at the warehouse location. The total value of business personal property at the manufacturing facility is $20,000,000 (including machinery used in the manufacturing process). Lumber located at the warehouse/storage building fluctuates in value frequently, both due to the price of lumber and to frequent inventory changes. Currently, lumber on hand is valued at $700,000 and the equipment located at the warehouse has a schedule limit of $175,000.

WWP also owns a fleet of 100 delivery trucks, 50 of which are semi-trailer and tractor units. In addition, the president of WWP owns a 2024 Mercedes Benz GLA SUV, valued at $45,000. It is driven mainly for personal use and is titled in the name of WWP. The president's wife drives a 2005 Aston Martin DB12, valued at $240,000, which is also titled in the name of WWP. The last private passenger auto titled in the name of WWP is driven by the president's 18-year-old son, who works occasionally during the summer for WWP. He has had three speeding violations during the past three years, and he drives a 2016 Chevrolet Corvette Stingray Z51 LT2, valued at $40,000.

Western Wooden Products, Inc. Year-End Financial Statement

Income

Furniture Sales	$ 149,000,000
Excess Lumber Sales	$ 1,000,000
Gross Sales	$ 150,000,000

Less Cost of Goods Sold

Lumber Costs	$ 75,000,000
Furniture Damaged in Mfg Process	$ 500,000
Total Costs	$ 75,500,000
Gross Profit	$ 74,500,000

Operating Expenses

Insurance	$ 2,500,000
Utilities (Heat and Electric)	$ 1,000,000
Payroll	$ 25,250,000
Fixed Rents	$ 15,000,000
Taxes	$ 15,750,000
Total Expenses	$ 59,500,000
Net Profit	$ 15,000,000

Appendix

Case Analysis Questions

1. List some of the methods you can use to identify major risk exposures to Western Wooden Products, Inc. (WWP) and Products Building Leases, LLC (PBL).

2. What are some of the techniques/tools/methods that can be used to address risk exposures?

3. What services could a risk manager provide that would help WWP and PBL address risk?

4. Identify contractual risk management tools/techniques that a risk manager may use when reviewing contracts.

5. What are some reasons for carrying a high deductible?

6. How would you go about allocating the cost of risk for both WWP and PBL?

7. Explain the concept of enterprise risk management.

8. What are some of the reasons it makes sense to develop a risk management policy and procedures manual?

Case Analysis Worksheet*

Identify any type of exposure to loss based on the case study. Loss exposures may include Direct Property, Indirect Losses, General Liability, Human Resources & Employment Practices, Auto, Surety, Leases and Contracts.

Exposure Identified	Measurement Frequency or Severity	Recommended Treatment
	L M S	
	L M S	
	L M S	
	L M S	
	L M S	
	L M S	
	L M S	
	L M S	
	L M S	
	L M S	
	L M S	
	L M S	
	L M S	

Note: L = Low, M = Moderate, S = Severe

*Used with permission of the National Alliance for Insurance Education and Research

Appendix

Western Wooden Products, Inc. Year-End Financial Answers

1. **List some of the methods you can use to identify major risk exposures to WWP and PBL.**

    1. Standardized surveys and questionnaires.
    2. Financial statements.
    3. Other records and files.
    4. Activities flow charts.
    5. Personal inspections.
    6. Discussions.

2. **What are some of the techniques/tools/methods that can be used to address risk exposures?**

    1. Exposure avoidance.
    2. Loss prevention.
    3. Loss reduction.
    4. Segregating exposures.
    5. Contractual transfer.
    6. Retention.

3. **What services could a risk manager provide that would help WWP and PBL address risk?**

    A risk manager can:

    a. Develop and communicate risk management policies.
    b. Provide communication: internal and external.

c. Conduct risk identification surveys.

d. Arrange risk financing (including insurance placement).

e. Manage litigation in conjunction with Claims/Legal Department.

f. Investigate accidents.

g. Implement loss control program.

h. Provide contractual analysis and review leases.

i. Determine cost of risk.

j. Prepare allocations to cost centers.

k. Audit existing insurance/self-insurance programs in the property, casualty, employee benefits and pension areas

l. Design insurance programs, including both primary and excess layers.

m. Prepare specifications for insurance programs being bid, as well as an evaluation of the responses to the specifications.

n. Analyze the various funding alternatives for any desired lines of insurance to be studied.

o. Participate in due diligence analysis related to mergers and acquisitions.

p. Design, implement and monitor claims handling and loss control procedures.

q. Conduct feasibility studies for captives and association-owned insurance companies.

r. Review, analyze and monitor overall risk management department operations, program results and effectiveness.

s. Coordinate risk management policies with organizational mission and goals.

t. Facilitate the development or purchase of a Risk Management Information System (RMIS).

4. **Identify contractual risk management tools/techniques that a risk manager may use when reviewing contracts.**

   1. Hold harmless agreement

   2. Indemnity agreement

   3. Exculpatory clause

5. **What are some reasons for carrying a high deductible?**

   a. A credit is applied by the insurance company that lowers the price you pay for insurance.

   b. By carrying a high deductible, you are showing the insurance company that you are willing to bear part of the risk of loss to your buildings and business personal property. This makes insurance company underwriters more comfortable with accepting your account and may result in an overall lower price for your insurance.

   c. Losses incurred below your deductible threshold may be eligible for deduction on your corporate federal income taxes.

6. **How would you go about allocating the cost of risk for WWP and PBL?**

   a. Decide whether you will use an exposure-based allocation, experience-based allocation, or a combination of the two methods

   b. Include the following costs in your allocation system:

      1. Risk management departmental costs

      2. Outside services

      3. Retained losses (passive and active)

      4. Insurance premiums

      5. Other considerations (indirect costs)

7. **Explain the concept of Enterprise Risk Management**

    a. Enterprise Risk Management focuses on all risks that impact the company. A loose definition of Enterprise Risk Management is: a basis for handling all the risks facing an organization, whether insurable or not.

    b. Enterprise Risk Management describes an approach to risk management. It involves a wide range of tools and methodologies all designed to understand the relationship between an organization's risk profile and its impact on earnings and shareholder value.

    c. Broadly speaking, the four (4) main categories of enterprise risk are:

    1. Hazard/event
    2. Financial
    3. Strategic
    4. Operational

8. **What are some of the reasons it makes sense to develop a risk management policy and procedures manual?**

    The purpose of a policies and procedures manual is to:

    1. Reaffirm corporate policies.
    2. Communicate risk management policy.
    3. Communicate senior management's support for the risk management program, which includes the risk management policy, the risk management mission statement, and the risk management policy and procedures manual.
    4. Define responsibility and authority.
    5. Familiarize personnel with exposures and procedures (risk management policy statements).
    6. Provide a convenient reference–i.e., a "How To" guide.

Appendix

7. Convey a positive image of the risk management department.

8. Detail policies and procedures in selection of third-party service providers.

Sample 2: Insurance Proposal Comparison Worksheet

Caution: do not use this exact worksheet to depict your unique insurance related exposures without modification. It is provided here only as a sample to assist you in arranging how your information might be structured before sending it to an insurance agent to obtain a quote, and/or how you might summarize information contained in quotes that you receive.

This sample worksheet contains a simple illustration of how information received from insurance companies quoting a businessowners policy (BOP) might look. Keep in mind that actual BOP comparison worksheets, other types of business insurance worksheets, as well as personal insurance worksheets, will look different than the sample provided due to the unique nature of different insurance situations.

INSURANCE PROPOSAL COMPARISON

Insurance Company Name:	Incumbent Carrier	Quoted Carrier #1	Quoted Carrier #2	Quoted Carrier #3
EFFECTIVE DATE:				
SCOPE OF BUSINESS OPERATIONS				
COVERAGE		LIMIT:	LIMIT:	LIMIT:
Buildings				
Loc. 1				
Personal Property				
Loc. 1				
Business Income and Extra Expense				
Loc. 1				
Description of Locations Covered				
Loc. 1				
Perils Insured Against				
Deductible				
Valuation				
Coinsurance				
Agreed Value (Suspends Coinsurance)				

Appendix

	Incumbent Carrier	Quoted Carrier #1	Quoted Carrier #2	Quoted Carrier #3
PROPERTY				
Debris Removal				
Newly Acquired or Constructed Property				
Buildings				
Business Personal Property				
Number of Days to Report				
Outdoor Property Limit				
Mechanical Breakdown				
Signs				
Accounts Receivable				
Valuable Papers				
On Premises				
Off Premises				
Crime				
Money & Securities: Inside Limit				
Money & Securities: Outside Limit				
Transit				
Computer Coverage				

	Incumbent Carrier	Quoted Carrier #1	Quoted Carrier #2	Quoted Carrier #3
Non-Owned Tools and Equipment				
Personal Effects				
Water Back-Up/ Sump Pump Overflow				
Changes in Temperature/ Humidity				
Off-Premises Utility Failure				
Ordinance or Law				
ADDITONAL COVERAGES				
Earthquake Coverage				
Flood Coverage				
ERISA Employee Dishonesty				
Employee Dishonesty				
Employment Related Practices Liability				
Employee Benefits Liability				
COMMERCIAL AUTO LIABILITY				
Liability Insurance				
Medical Payments				

	Incumbent Carrier	Quoted Carrier #1	Quoted Carrier #2	Quoted Carrier #3
Uninsured Motorists				
Underinsured Motorists				
Other Than Collision Coverage				
Collision Coverage				
Hired Auto Physical Damage				
Fellow Employee Exclusion				
BUSINESS LIABILITY				
MEDICAL PAYMENTS				
Endorsements Included				
Voluntary Property Damage				
Deletion of Fellow Employee Exclusion				
Stop Gap Liability				
Employees as Additional Insureds				

	Incumbent Carrier	Quoted Carrier #1	Quoted Carrier #2	Quoted Carrier #3
WORKER'S COMPENSATION				
Coverage A				
Coverage B				
Applicable States				
Rating Basis Classification				
Classifications				
Experience Modification Factor				
Dividend Offered				
Exclusions and Endorsements				
Excess Coverage (Umbrella)				
Retained Limit				
Exclusions and Endorsements				

QUOTED PREMIUMS:	Expiring Policies	Quoted Carrier #1	Quoted Carrier #2	Quoted Carrier #3
Businessowners' Policy (BOP)				
Inland Marine				
Commercial Automobile Liability				
Excess Liability				
Worker's Compensation				
Employment Practices Liability				
ACCOUNT TOTAL:				

Index

A

accident, 22, 28, 31-32, 49-50

accidents, 27, 31, 37, 47, 134

accommodation, 62-63

accommodations, 87

account, 27, 30, 42, 63, 82-85, 95, 96-99, 102-103, 115-116, 120, 135

accounts, 16, 38-39, 53, 65, 83, 86, 102-103, 121

action, 3, 20, 32, 36, 49, 58, 68, 71-74, 107

actions, 3, 30, 62, 69, 72-75, 87, 114

actuarial, 46-48

actuaries, 33, 46

actuary, 49

Actuary, 15, 45-46

adhesion, 26

adjuster, 24, 26, 33-37, 52, 73, 75, 116

adjusters, 23-24, 26, 29-30, 33-37, 52, 59, 67-68, 75, 98, 107

adjusting, 24

adverse, 1, 2, 15, 32, 37, 72, 83

adversely, 12, 18, 20

advice, 21-22, 29, 35-36, 68, 72

advising, 27

advocates, 68

agencies, 8-10, 12, 17-18, 44, 51, 56, 67, 82, 86-88, 91, 94-95, 97-98, 102, 109, 119-121, 124

agency, 8-10, 12, 16, 18, 20, 40, 48, 56, 72, 86-88, 95-97, 99, 101-103, 121

agent, 8-10, 13, 16-22, 29-30, 33, 35-36, 38-39, 42, 52, 68, 70, 72-73, 76- 79, 81-82, 87-88, 91, 93-102, 105, 121, 123-124, 137

Agent, 20, 72, 75-79, 90, 101

agents, 8-11, 13, 16-18, 20-22, 29, 33, 39, 53, 72-73, 82, 90, 91, 94, 96, 98, 101-102, 120-121

agreement, 4, 63, 103, 112, 135

agreements, 12, 62, 108

aleatory, 73

ambiguities, 6, 26

ambiguity, 54

analysis, 3, 37, 40, 69, 70, 108-109, 134

Analysis, 69, 131-132

analyze, 3, 46, 69, 134

Analyze, 134

analyzes, 106, 109

analyzing, 2

ancillary, 42, 46, 63, 111

Appendix, 97, 106, 127

application, 9, 22, 38, 76, 107

Application, 76

applications, 22, 37, 121, 124

artificial intelligence, 116-117, 120

attorney, 22, 25-26, 33, 35-36, 39, 50, 74-75, 78, 100

Attorney, 11

attorneys, 24, 36-37, 45-46, 51, 60, 72, 74

audit, 41, 44, 52, 108

Audit, 15, 40, 45, 52, 134

auditable, 40-41

audited, 40

Auditors, 52

audits, 69

authority, 38, 85, 118, 136

avoidance, 3, 133

B

bad faith, 73-75

bias, 33, 116

bid, 11-12, 95, 107, 134

bidding, 12, 95

bid-rigging, 11-12

bids, 11

book of business, 12, 18, 47, 62-63, 86, 103

bordereau, 62

Bordereau, 63

breach, 74

broad, 16, 105, 120

broaden, 33

broader, 21, 64, 101, 119

broker, 10-11, 13, 18, 101-102, 107

brokerage, 8, 11-12, 101-103, 120

brokers, 8, 10-13, 18, 95, 101, 102, 106, 108

business, 2-5, 7, 9, 11-12, 15, 17-20, 26-27, 29, 32-33, 37-44, 46-47, 49, 52, 56, 58, 60-64, 67-69, 76-80, 82-88, 91, 95-96, 99, 101-103, 105-108, 116, 118-121, 127-129, 135, 137

Business, 40, 76, 79, 83, 85-86, 127, 129, 138-139

C

Cancellation, 79

cancelled, 29, 124-125

capacity, 36, 55

captive, 9, 16, 70

Captive, 18

captives, 109, 134

care, custody, control, 26-27, 38, 74-75, 116

Index

carrier, 12, 19, 20, 34-37, 39, 44, 47, 50, 57, 63, 65, 73, 77-80, 83, 85, 97, 99, 107, 116, 125

Carrier, 7, 51, 138-139, 143

carriers, 5, 8-9, 11-12, 31, 38, 53, 54, 57-58, 64-68, 73, 75, 91, 95, 98, 112, 114-116, 120

casualty, 69, 95, 102, 115, 134

Casualty, 24

catastrophe, 115-116, 118

catastrophes, 58, 62, 114-115, 124

catastrophic, 27, 62, 69, 81, 114-115, 125

CAT bond, 115

claim, 20, 23-37, 42, 46, 49, 52, 58, 67-69, 73-75, 77-79, 108, 112, 116

Claim, 77- 79

claimant, 23, 25

claimants, 25, 74

claims, 3-4, 6-7, 12, 16, 23-36, 38, 43, 45-47, 49-54, 56, 59, 62, 67, 70, 73-75, 95, 97, 105, 107-109, 112, 116, 118, 120, 123, 125, 134

Claims, 15, 23-25, 27, 29-30, 34, 69, 74-75, 134

class, 42, 48, 83, 96, 116

Class, 39, 128

classification, 40, 44, 115

client, 19-21, 33, 37, 82, 101, 103, 107

clients, 8, 10, 13, 19, 36, 41, 53, 68, 89, 95, 97, 99, 101-103, 107

climate change, 114

climate-related risks, 114

commercial, 33, 38, 39-40, 46, 76, 82-84, 86, 101-102, 119

Commercial, 39-40, 78, 84, 143

commercial package policies (CPP), 119

commission, 12, 18-19, 101-103

Commissioner of Insurance, 35, 98

commissions, 11-12, 18, 21, 33, 40, 72, 86, 101-103, 121, 124

communication, 35, 72, 120, 133

compensation, 19, 40, 43-44, 46, 50-51, 85, 102, 121

Compensation, 24, 40, 44, 108, 143

competition, 47, 54, 119

consult, 24, 75

consultant, 21, 26, 35-37, 69-70, 86, 90, 96, 101-102, 107, 127

Consultant, 77, 100, 127

consultants, 37, 68-69, 90, 101

Consultants, 68

consulting, 29, 69, 95

consumer, 7, 10, 16-17, 26-27, 39, 57, 68, 81, 87, 98, 120, 124-125

consumers, 6, 11-12, 39, 57, 64, 82, 101, 116, 119, 120-121

147

Consumers, 17, 27, 120

contingency, 20, 36, 124

contingent, 11-12, 18-19

contract, 6, 9, 18, 23, 26, 33-34, 53, 61, 67, 73-74, 112

contracts, 8, 10, 16, 56, 60, 73, 101, 108, 110, 118-119, 131, 135

Contracts, 132

contractual, 4, 72, 112, 131, 134-135

Contractual, 4, 133

contractually, 18

cost, 2, 6, 8, 12, 22, 25, 27, 31, 33, 41-42, 44, 59-60, 63-65, 77, 79, 87-88, 90, 92, 94, 109, 115, 125, 128, 131, 134-135

Cost, 77, 130

costs, 41-43, 60, 64, 71, 76, 83-84, 92, 109, 115, 135

Costs, 130

court, 5, 24, 26, 28, 46, 53, 71, 73-75

coverage, 4, 13, 16, 19-22, 24, 26, 27-29, 33, 35, 39, 53-54, 61, 65, 68-69, 72-73, 75-80, 82, 90-91, 96, 98, 100, 107-108, 112, 119

Coverage, 39, 75- 77, 93-94, 139-142

coverages, 11-12, 16, 19, 21-22, 25-26, 34-35, 38, 54, 58, 64, 72, 76, 87, 90-93, 95-98, 100-101, 119, 123-124

Coverages, 21, 93

covered, 4, 6, 23, 26, 33-34, 42, 68, 74-75, 81, 115

credit, 41, 47, 82, 84-85, 99, 135

customer, 6-7, 9, 15-16, 20-21, 25, 34, 38, 41-42, 44, 54, 72-73, 83, 86-88, 96, 127-128

Customer, 76-77, 120

customers, 8-13, 16-17, 19-21, 23, 25, 47, 54, 59, 71, 82, 87, 95, 120-121, 125

D

damage, 4, 25-28, 30, 38, 43, 57, 78, 80, 112-113, 116

Damage, 78-79, 141

damaged, 28, 79

Damaged, 130

damages, 25, 30, 42, 46, 49-50, 62, 72, 74, 78-79, 114

Damages, 76, 79

debit, 84-85

defendant, 74, 76,-78

defense, 5, 32, 46, 72-73, 78

Defense, 75

denial, 30, 35, 74, 78-79

Denial, 78-79

denied, 29, 33, 35, 74-80, 124

denies, 25

deny, 6, 25, 73

Department of Insurance, 27, 48, 57, 98

direct writer, 8, 9, 16, 56

discrimination, 46, 116

discriminatory, 38

distribution, 5, 8-10, 15-17, 119, 124

distributor, 83, 121

dividend, 7, 85

dividends, 85

dual fiduciary responsibility, 10, 33, 101

duty of buyers, 20

E

employee, 9, 34, 43, 46, 51, 79, 134

Employee, 140-141

employees, 9, 15, 26, 34, 42-43, 52, 59, 68

employer, 26, 51, 86

endorsement, 26-27

Endorsement, 76

endorsements, 39, 55, 93

Errors and Omissions, 72

exception, 38, 62, 85, 116

exceptions, 38, 82

excess, 64, 74, 92, 134

Excess, 92, 130, 142-143

excluded, 62

excluding, 19, 97, 102

exclusion, 26, 62, 76

Exclusion, 76, 141

exclusions, 4, 22, 27, 39, 42, 62, 63, 93, 98

exclusive agency, 8, 16

experience, 5, 17, 26, 35-36, 45-48, 58, 65, 84-86, 100, 102, 109, 135

Experience, 83, 85, 142

expert, 5, 22, 28, 36, 69, 72, 76-77

experts, 46, 63, 124

exposure, 40, 41, 63, 69, 81, 98, 108, 115, 132, 135

Exposure, 69, 132, 133

exposures, 40, 43, 63, 69, 81, 99, 100, 108-109, 112, 114, 127, 131-133, 136-137

Exposures, 4

external sales, 15-16

F

facultative, 62-64

fiduciary, 8, 10, 16, 33, 101, 106

file-and-use, 48

fraud, 52, 53

function, 39, 105

functions, 16, 108, 116

Functions, 15

future of insurance, 117

G

general liability, 26, 39, 46, 82-83, 95

guaranteed, 85, 116

guideline, 24, 37-38, 46, 52, 82, 84, 119

H

handling, 24, 28, 30, 36, 74-75, 79, 96, 109, 134, 136

Handling, 78

hard market, 64

holdback, 11

hold harmless agreement, 4

homeowner, 30, 31, 38, 48, 57, 81, 93-94, 101

homeowners, 27, 31, 37, 47-48, 53, 82, 94-95, 114

I

IBNR, 47

identification, 2, 108-109, 127, 134

impact, 12, 15, 18, 20, 29, 42, 45, 47, 56-57, 61, 86, 111, 114, 117, 125, 136

Impact, 64, 77

implementation, 64, 69-70, 108, 118

incentives, 18

Indemnity agreement, 135

independent, 8,-10, 16, 20, 34, 45, 56, 90, 94, 112

Independent, 8, 18

information technology, 27, 54-55

injuries, 22, 27, 30, 43, 46, 49, 118

insurance, 3-13, 15-102, 105-109, 111-112, 114-121, 123-125, 127, 134-135, 137

insurance agent duties, 21

insurance brokerage, 11

insurance companies, 4-12, 15, 18-19, 24, 27-29, 31-34, 38-39, 41-42, 45-48, 51, 53-59, 61-62, 64-65, 67, 72-73, 75, 81, 83-84, 86-91, 94-99, 101, 106, 109, 112, 116-117, 119-120, 121, 124-125, 127, 134, 137

insurance company, 5-9, 11-12, 15-16, 18-20, 23-27, 29-30, 32,-35, 37-64, 67-70, 73-74, 77-79, 81-84, 86-88, 91, 9-102, 112, 118-119, 121, 124, 135

insurance leads, 17

Insurance Proposal Comparison Worksheet, 127, 137

insure, 19-20, 43, 61, 63, 81, 83-84, 86, 99-100, 112

insured, 21-22, 28, 34-35, 46, 48-49, 63, 73-75, 77-78, 83, 100, 110, 112, 128

Insured, 78-79, 138

insureds, 6, 24, 30, 31, 35, 45-47, 65, 72, 75, 112, 114

insurer, 9, 20, 28, 42, 47, 64-65, 73-74, 81, 84, 87, 99, 112

Insurer, 77, 86

insurers, 5-6, 9, 30, 31, 38, 48-49, 53, 62, 65, 100, 108, 114-115

interest, 1, 11-13, 16, 19-20, 25, 27, 33, 46, 67, 77, 82, 86-87, 106-107, 114-115

Interest, 77

internal audit, 52, 108

internal sales, 15

IRPM, 84-85

J

judgment, 30, 38, 40, 50, 71, 83-84

K

kickbacks, 52

L

Law of Large Numbers, 81

legal, 4, 10-11, 16, 21, 33, 37, 45, 49-50, 52, 54, 71-73

Legal, 15, 45, 108, 134

legal liability, 4

legally, 10, 20, 27, 51, 118

legislation, 24, 56-57, 118

liabilities, 47

liability, 4, 26, 27, 31, 33, 38-39, 43-44, 46, 48-49, 52, 76, 82-83, 92-93, 95, 124

Liability, 40, 76, 78-79, 132, 140-141, 143

liable, 27, 30, 32, 118

licensed, 8, 19, 68, 96

limit, 20, 58, 63, 67, 75, 77, 92, 94, 100, 112, 118, 129

limitations, 4, 22, 27, 93, 98, 116

limits, 4, 25, 42, 46, 58, 64, 69, 72, 74-75, 77-79, 92-93, 115-116, 123-124

Limits, 21, 79

loss control, 42-44, 69, 95, 108-109, 134

loss ratio, 12, 18, 32

M

management, 2-3, 24, 27, 38, 42-43, 47-48, 52, 54-56, 58-60, 65, 68-69, 82, 90, 105-110, 115, 127, 131, 133-137

manufacturer, 5, 8, 19, 40, 42, 55, 71

manufacturers, 5-6, 8, 43

Manufacturers, 8, 87

manufacturing, 42, 107, 128-129

marketing, 8-9, 15-16, 34, 46-47, 54, 59, 69, 100

material change in risk, 30

method, 3-4, 8-9, 16-17, 38, 91, 97, 115, 120

methods, 3, 8-9, 16-17, 62, 90, 114, 131, 133, 135

morale hazard, 37-38

moral hazard, 37

mutual, 1, 6, 7, 119-120

Mutual, 7, 9

N

negligence, 49, 51, 72, 73

Negligence, 78-79

negligent, 27, 46, 49-51, 72

negotiate, 88, 118

negotiated, 62

Negotiates, 108

negotiations, 25, 50, 75, 118

negotiators, 87

non-auditable, 41

O

Occupational Safety and Health Administration (OSHA), 44

occur, 3-4, 27, 30-31, 43, 61-62, 73, 92, 100, 105, 111, 114, 116, 123-124

occurred, 3, 22, 52, 76-79, 111, 114

occurrence, 4, 11, 30, 51

occurrences, 59

occurring, 3, 22, 37, 64, 114, 119

occurs, 4, 23, 28, 43, 49, 67, 68-69, 81, 112, 115

Omissions, 72

P

Parametric Insurance, 112

personal insurance, 29, 31-32, 91, 94, 96, 101, 119, 137

plaintiff, 33, 36, 72,-74, 76-80

Plaintiff, 77-78

plaintiffs, 22, 36, 73, 76-77

policies, 4, 6, 8-12, 16-19, 21, 23, 25, 28-29, 31-32, 34, 37-41, 43, 46-47, 49, 53, 55, 56, 61, 63,-65, 73, 76-77, 81-83, 85-86, 88-92, 94-97, 99-100, 102, 108-110, 112, 115, 119-121, 124-125, 133-137

policy, 4-8, 11-13, 15, 17, 19-33, 35, 38-42, 46-47, 50, 53, 55-56, 58-59, 61-62, 64, 67, 69, 72-82, 88, 90-96, 98-101, 103, 107, 109, 112, 116, 118-119, 124-125, 131, 136-137

Policy, 12, 15, 26, 33, 39, 55, 76, 78-79, 143

policyholder, 6, 23, 26-28, 31-32, 34-35, 41, 45-46, 49-50, 62, 67-69, 73-74, 86

policyholders, 6-7, 9, 23-24, 27, 30, 47, 51, 53, 57, 64-65, 68, 98, 125

policy services, 116

Index

predictive modeling, 115

prevention, 3, 43, 133

pricing authority, 38

primary, 4-5, 8, 58, 62, 72, 102, 107, 115, 134

prior-approval, 48

process, 2, 5, 12, 13, 16-17, 19, 20-22, 25, 27, 29, 33-35, 37-38, 42, 43, 48, 50, 55, 58, 63, 69, 71, 83, 91, 95-96, 98, 101, 105, 116, 129

Process, 2, 17, 50, 130

procuring, 20

product development, 6, 53-54, 55

product development department, 6

Products Building Leases, LLC, 128, 131

Profit, 130

programming, 55-56

proposal, 127

proposals, 12, 20, 96

punitive damages, 72, 74

Q

quality control, 39-40, 116

quote, 19-20, 82, 90, 92, 98, 124, 137

quoted, 20, 97, 102

quotes, 12-13, 19, 65, 92-94, 124, 137

R

rate, 1, 7, 31, 38, 40-41, 46-47, 48, 49, 57, 82, 83, 84

Rate, 39, 47, 57

Ratemaking, 47

rates, 29, 31, 33, 39-40, 48, 53, 58, 83-85, 115

Rates, 39-40

rating methodology, 38

ratio, 12, 18, 32, 82

recommendation, 54, 107

recommendations, 42, 52, 69, 108

Recommendations, 69

reduction, 3, 39, 65, 102, 133

referral, 17

referrals, 17

Referrals, 17, 91

referred, 6, 9-10, 16, 21, 47, 49-50, 91, 105, 112

reinsurance, 61-65, 82, 115

Reinsurance, 61-64

reinsure, 62-63

reinsured, 62

reinsurer, 61-63, 84

reinsurers, 62, 115

Reinsurers, 61

RISC Analyzer, 99, 100

risk, 1-4, 30, 32, 37, 39, 41-43, 58, 62-64, 68-70, 75, 81-84, 90, 105-110, 112, 114-116, 127, 131, 133-137

Risk, 1-3, 24, 57, 69, 77, 105-107, 118, 127, 134-136

risk control, 3-4

risk identification, 2, 109, 134

risk management, 2, 42, 68-69, 90, 105-110, 115, 127, 131, 133-137

Risk Management, 24, 105, 134, 136

risk modeling, 114-116

risks, 1-4, 30, 38, 41, 63, 99-100, 114-116, 127, 136

S

Safety Engineering, 41

sales, 8-9, 15-20, 40-41, 48, 56, 82-83, 87, 90, 121, 128

Sales, 16-17, 128, 130

salespersons, 16-17, 102, 119, 128

Segregation of Exposures, 4

settlement, 25, 29, 34, 45, 75, 108

settlements, 24

severity, 31, 43-44, 114-116

Severity, 132

soft market, 64

specialized, 36, 69, 75, 121

Specialized, 69, 101

specific rate, 40, 41

standards, 11, 24, 64, 108, 115, 119

stock, 1, 6-8, 58, 65, 120

submission, 38

subrogation, 49-51

Subrogation, 15, 45, 49-51

summary of insurance coverages and limits, 93

surcharges, 28

surplus, 49, 57-58, 62, 64-65

T

Terrorism Risk Insurance Program Reauthorization Act (TRIPRA), 118

tiered, 38

tiers, 82

tort, 74

transfer, 3-4, 69, 100, 105, 108-109, 115, 133

Treaties, 62

treaty, 62-64, 115

Treaty, 62

U

umbrella, 8, 58, 92, 94, 124

underwriter, 24, 38, 40, 62-63, 82-85, 116

Underwriter, 24

underwriters, 24, 26, 32, 34, 37, 42, 46, 59, 63-64, 82-84, 107, 115, 135

Underwriters, 31, 37-38, 63, 84-85

underwriting, 27-29, 37-38, 40, 42, 52, 54, 56, 59, 64, 81-82, 85, 86, 107, 112, 115-116, 118-120

Underwriting, 15, 24, 37, 47

Unfair Claims Settlement Practices Act, 24-25

unilateral, 26, 73

Uninsured, 77, 141

V

violation, 31, 48

violations, 32, 37, 129

Voluntary Property Damage, 141

W

Western Wooden Products, Inc., 128, 130-131, 133

Wisconsin Compensation Rating Bureau (WCRB), 44

worker's compensation, 40, 43-44, 46, 51, 85, 102

wrongdoing, 52, 71, 74-75, 79

If More Help is Needed

Now that you have read Inside the Insurance Industry-Fourth Edition, are you still confused in certain areas, or are there particular things that you would like more help with?

If so, here are options for your consideration:

1. For individuals and small businesses who wish to identify your specific risk exposures on your own, and to address these potential shortcomings with your insurance agent, visit our website at: https://www.riscanalyzer.com (discussed in Chapter 9).

2. For affluent individuals, family offices, and large, complex commercial businesses that would like help from an unbiased, independent, fee-only property and casualty consultant to confidentially discuss areas such as:

    - A review of your existing insurance and risk management programs

    - Securing competitive insurance program proposals

    - Obtaining ad hoc assistance, as needed

    Contact Risk & Insurance Services Consulting, LLC via email at riscllc@riscllc.com.

3. For assistance with either plaintiff or defense insurance litigation support and expert witness services, contact Kevin L. Glaser, CPCU, CIC, SCLA, ARM, AAI, AIC, ARM-P, AIS, via email at riscllc@riscllc.com.

Thank you for reading this book and please remember to leave a review on the site of your choice if you enjoyed it!

www.ingramcontent.com/pod-product-compliance
Lightning Source LLC
Chambersburg PA
CBHW070358240426
43671CB00013BA/2560